The First Freedom

*Considerations on Church and State
in the United States*

WILFRID PARSONS, S.J.

THE
FIRST
FREEDOM

*Considerations on Church and State
in the United States*

WITH A FOREWORD BY
MOST REVEREND FRANCIS P. KEOUGH
ARCHBISHOP OF BALTIMORE

THE DECLAN X. McMULLEN COMPANY, INC.

IMPRIMI POTEST
   David Nugent, S.J.
   Provincial

NIHIL OBSTAT
   John Courtney Murray, S.J.
   Censor deputatus

IMPRIMATUR
   ✠ Patrick A. O'Boyle
   Archbishop of Washington

APRIL 10, 1948

Acknowledgments

THE AUTHOR wishes to pay a special debt of
gratitude to the late Archbishop James H. Ryan,
D.D., of Omaha, Nebraska, Episcopal Chairman of
the Department of Education, National Catholic
Welfare Conference, at whose suggestion the writing of this book was undertaken, and whose constant encouragement helped it to fulfillment.

He acknowledges special indebtedness to Dr.
Richard J. Purcell, of The Catholic University of
America, who has made available in manuscript his
wide, though unpublished, research in early constitutional history, which, with his permission, has
been utilized in the first four chapters, and which,
it is hoped, will soon appear in book form.

He also is grateful to George E. Reed, Esq., of the
Legal Department of the N.C.W.C., upon whose
fundamental research on this question he has constantly relied.

He also wishes to thank the following: Rev. Francis J. Connell, C.SS.R., Rev. Joseph T. Durkin, S.J., Rev. Gustav Gundlach, S.J., Rev. Dr. Jerome D. Hannan, Rev. Robert C. Hartnett, S.J., James V. Hayes, Esq., Rev. Joseph Lecler, S.J., Rev. William E. McManus, Rev. Moorhouse F. X. Millar, S.J., Rev. John Courtney Murray, S.J., Rev. Francis J. Powers, C.S.V., Dr. Heinrich Rommen, Very Rev. Paul Tanner, Rev. Gerald G. Walsh, S.J., and Dr. Francis Wilson, all of whom read this book in manuscript, and many of whom supplied valuable material and suggestions.

Needless to say, the opinions expressed here do not necessarily represent those whom I have named.

W. P.

Contents

Foreword

IT HAS become a matter of grave concern to many Americans that a rising tide of secularism threatens the traditional foundations on which human life in America has always been based. In their Statement of November, 1947, the Administrative Board of the National Catholic Welfare Confer ence seriously warned all believers that this phenomenon is the most menacing portent of our time. The warning has been echoed by many of our Protestant and Jewish fellow citizens.

It is, of course, a common temptation of our human nature to put the purely temporal interests of man above the spiritual in our daily life. All moralists have freely recognized this temptation. The secularism of which we speak, however, is something far more serious than a failing derived from the frailty of human nature. This secularism is a conscious, intellectual movement which explicitly teaches that this failing is the only normal and acceptable state of man. It holds that its opposite, the supernatural viewpoint, is artificial and thus harmful.

What is even more alarming is that this doctrine, which is new to America and may well prove its undoing, is now being extended from what was a purely private viewpoint to the status of an officially recognized American theory of state. We are being told that the American democracy has no truly religious origins, but is founded on a merely secularist and unreligious view of the nature of man. Yet, as Father Parsons shows in these pages, from the very beginnings of our political system a religious motivation ran all through our public life. The Declaration of Independence, the Constitutional Convention, the States' ratifying Conventions, the First Congress, and all but a very few of our Founding Fathers took the view that "religion and morality" are the very foundation stones of our American system, as George Washington pointed out in his Farewell Address. On many occasions, our Supreme Court has declared that this is a nation which has its moral foundation deep in the Gospel tradition. Every successive Congress has in its legislation openly recognized the claims of religion. Presidents of the United States repeatedly have acknowledged the Almighty in their messages and proclamations. On the other hand, until very recent times, no one has seriously challenged the right of the religious forces of our country to influence by their moral and religious teachings the course of our national life. State and church are societies distinct in their purpose and operation, but their co-operation for the common good has always been a distinctive mark of American civilization.

In very recent years, this whole American body of tradition has been under severe attack. Catholics, naturally, along with many others, have viewed this new development with much alarm. Even more portentous, however, is the fact that many professing Christians have, wittingly or unwittingly, taken sides with the secularists in their campaign to drive religion out of public life under the specious pretext of separation of church and state.

This disturbing situation has, in its turn, given rise to another and perhaps more acute development, and that is a divisive conflict between Catholics and other professing Christians. This conflict, like many others of its kind, has arisen out of misunderstandings and has caused other misunderstandings in its turn. There are ominous signs of further bitter religious animosities growing out of this conflict, yet nothing should be clearer than that moderate Protestants and Catholics stand on common ground in their attitude toward the inroads of secularism as an instrument of driving religious influences out of American life.

It seems that it ought to be possible to find an approach which would lead to an understanding based on the American theory of state. Separation of church and state, as understood in our history, is derived from the First Amendment to the United States Constitution. The historical approach, therefore, would seem to be the most promising one, since it will tell us what was in the minds of the Founding Fathers when they forbade the Federal Government to establish a national church or to invade the sacred rights of conscience. This is the approach which Father Parsons has taken in this book. This seems all the more necessary because several recent events have shown that the historical background of religious freedom in this country is either unknown or gravely misunderstood.

The Founding Fathers were attempting a new experiment, not only in the general field of democratic government, but also in the more restricted one of church-state relations. That this experiment was successful is proved not only in our history of national stability, but also in the religious peace which with few interruptions we have enjoyed in this country—two characteristics which we are rather proud of possessing where many other nations have not been able to maintain or achieve them. In the past, we have usually in the end settled our differences by amicable agreement on the basis of reason, and not of passion, and there is no reason why this should not happen again once all the facts in the case are fully known and understood.

It was perhaps not surprising that the school question would become involved in the dispute over the meaning of separation of church and state. Here again, however, the historical approach should help to clear up many misunderstandings, not only with regard to the intent of our Constitution as to schools in general, but also to the nature of the public service which the Catholic parochial schools render to the nation. The liberty and equality which, as Father Parsons shows, were the true aim of our Constitutional provisions on religion in general should, in all fairness and equity, apply to schools in which religion is an integral part of their plan of education.

I share the hope expressed by Father Parsons that this book, while it may arouse discussion, may also lead to understanding and agreement even among a large section of our population which does not profess the Catholic religion. The troubled state of our modern world, and in particular the large place which our country is called on to occupy in the pacification of minds, demand that we should not divide our forces at home in this critical age. May Almighty God in His Providence bring us all to a final happy conclusion of charity and peace!

✠FRANCIS P. KEOUGH, D.D.
Archbishop of Baltimore
Chairman, Education Department,
N.C.W.C.

The First Freedom

Chapter One

Introduction to the Problem

THIS book is addressed to all Americans, of any or of no faith, who believe in the American constitutional principle of religious liberty. It is frankly written from the Catholic point of view, but also from that of Americans who are at the same time Catholics and who sincerely accept the constitutional and legal arrangements under which those of differing faiths so happily live together in this country.

Its purpose is to propose to our fellow countrymen for their consideration a growing and serious problem which involves the whole question of the relations of church and state in the United States.

The problem has been raised in various connections: free bus transportation for parochial-school children as well as for those of public schools; free textbooks for parochial-school children; released time from public schools for religious instruction; the NYA and Veterans' Bill of Rights funds for students at church schools; Bible reading, prayers, and the singing of Christmas carols in public schools; tax exemption of church-owned property; Federal aid to parochial schools; the presence of Mr. Myron Taylor at the Vatican as the President's personal representative. The most frequent discussions of the problem have centered about education.

The educational aspect of church-state relations is caused by this simple fact: the presence of some 2,400,000 Catholic children in separate elementary schools in the general public-education system of the country. These children are sons and daughters of American citizens who send their offspring to Catholic parochial schools in obedience to a double obligation: the State laws prescribing compulsory education of children up to a certain age; and the laws of the Catholic Church which lay down that religion is an essential part of the school education of a child of God.

The parochial schools, then, have a double aspect: in their secular aspect they are subject to the approval of the respective county or State boards of education which have competence in this field; they are also subject to Catholic diocesan supervision, which is authorized to see that the requirements of the Catholic Church are met as regards the teaching of religion. The diocesan supervision is, of course, also charged with the duty of making sure that these schools fully meet the educational standards established by the public authority.

The county, State, and regional educational bodies regard these schools as acceptable units of the public-education system. If the schools do not meet the requirements of these boards, the parents would not be considered as fulfilling their obligations under compulsory-education laws, and the schools themselves could not exist. If the schools do meet these requirements, then they are on an educational equality with those conducted by the city, county, or State, and should be so regarded.

It is important to make this point, because sometimes, even in legal arguments, parochial schools are confused with Sunday schools, weekday special classes in religion, Talmud Torah, and the like, in which the instruction is wholly religious. The Catholic parochial school is a true public school, in that its education fulfills all the secular demands made by the state; in addition, it illumines this secular education with religious motives and illustrations, in the belief that an education is not complete unless the pupil is presented with the whole of life, which includes an awareness of his obligations to God. That is why, in accord with the laws, and the principle of educational liberty, Catholics implement the state's educational system with schools in which the pupil's relation to God is included, in addition to instruction in the traditional secular subjects.

Here the problem begins: What may the state, and in particular the Federal Government, do under the Constitution with regard to such a school? Does the First Amendment forbid the Federal Government, and does the Fourteenth Amendment by implication forbid the States, to grant tax-supported benefits to any activity connected with the parochial school? Is there an American *principle* of separation of church and state, somehow connected with the Constitution, which operates to prohibit such grants? This is the first problem to be solved.

If there is no such constitutional prohibition, and if no principle operates in such a way, then a second question arises: If the state *may* grant its benefits to such a school, what is the nature and extent of any *duty* it may have toward it? Does the fact that the parochial school fulfills its duty to the state under the compulsory-education laws create a reciprocal duty on the part of the state to that school? Is there, or is there not, an obligation of the community as a whole to those millions of parents who, because of religious principle, consider that their obligations to both church and state are fulfilled by sending their children to parochial schools? Does the state's duty toward these of its children end at seeing that they receive an approved education in secular subjects?

As we shall see, there are some who believe that parents are delinquent in their duty to the state or recreant to democracy when they send their children to schools separate from the state-supported schools. They believe in a state monopoly of education. Fortunately, we have not come as a nation to accept the idea of such a monopoly, as the totalitarian nations have, and we believe we never will. Freedom of education is one of our fundamental rights.

At the other extreme, there are many believing Jews and Christians who hold in principle that young children should imbibe faith and hope in God, love of Him, along with their education; who are of the opinion that the family as it now is has not the capacity to inculcate such religious values, and hence are looking more and more to the school somehow to do it in their stead. One could quote many churchmen and educationists

7

on this point. Many of these, perhaps, look with a sort of friendly envy at the generosity of Catholics who spend so many millions a year in support of their double obligation to church and state.

Among these Jews and Christians, however, there looms one big obstacle to the attainment of this aspiration. If this is to be done in the public school, or if there is to be public support of private schools which teach religion, in either case there is a sort of civic scruple which would inhibit them from either course. The inhibition can be summed up in a single phrase: separation of church and state.

Now this phrase, as we shall see in the course of this discussion, has taken on many different meanings in its history. At the present day, it has probably reached its most extreme form, in that it would forbid every possible relationship between the state and any expression of religion. Its original meaning in this country—liberty and equality of all religions before the state—has often been overlooked. In some of its applications, it would even deny that very liberty and equality it was originally supposed to denote.

It has done particularly faithful service in the opposition to every form of state subsidy granted to any activity connected with the parochial school, even though that activity is secular in character. Many Protestant bodies have passed resolutions condemning such state support for Catholic schools as transgressing the "American principle of separation of church and state," even though in many cases the funds applied do not go to the schools themselves, but to the pupils or their parents. The issue has on at least three occasions reached the Supreme Court: one known as the Louisiana textbook case, a second as the New Jersey bus-fare case, and in both these cases the majority of the Court decided in favor of State subsidies for parochial school children. Another case, from Champaign, Illinois, concerning the teaching of religion on public-school premises, was decided adversely by the Supreme Court on March 8, 1948.

In the New Jersey case, the issue of separation of church and state was exhaustively argued both by the decision of the Court (Justice Black) and by the dissents of Justices Jackson and Rutledge. This was a case in which the New Jersey legislature authorized township boards of education to reimburse parents of both public-school and Catholic-school pupils for the bus fares they had expended to send them to school. In Ewing Township, a taxpayer, Arch Everson, argued that such payments were contrary to both the State and

Federal Constitutions. The Court of Errors and Appeals of New Jersey decided against Mr. Everson, and he carried his appeal to the Supreme Court of the United States. There, Justice Black, writing the majority decision, held that the Federal Constitution was not violated by the New Jersey law, and Justices Jackson, Rutledge, Frankfurter and Burton dissented, the two former writing opinions on their side.

Both the majority and the minority of the Court took serious cognizance of the relevance of separation of church and state, and in particular of the application of the First and Fourteenth Amendments to the United States Constitution, to the concept of separation.

In the Champaign case, where the issue was the use of public-school premises for the teaching of religion classes, the First Amendment was almost lost from sight, and in its stead was substituted a new concept of separation of church and state as set forth by Mr. Justice Black in the New Jersey decision. In the decision on this second case, also written by Mr. Black, his own definition of separation was used as the constitutional precedent, rather than the First Amendment itself, for a criterion in declaring unconstitutional the use of public-school buildings for religious teaching.

It becomes all the more necessary, therefore, to re-examine the real meaning of the First Amendment in history, law, and tradition. In view of Mr. Justice Reed's weighty dissent in the Champaign case, which was based squarely on the First Amendment itself and on its history, in forming our legal tradition, we are fully justified in calling for a review of the whole question. The following pages are intended as a contribution to this useful and now necessary end.

Those who oppose governmental action in the various cases involving church and state use two arguments, one drawn from the Constitution, the other, more broadly, from the American tradition. In each case, their argument can, for the sake of clarity, be reduced to a syllogism; that is, a conclusion drawn from two premises, one general and one particular. The argument runs thus:

"The United States Constitution (or the American tradition) imposes separation of church and state on both the nation and the States by virtue of the First and Fourteenth Amendments. But, Federal aid to parochial schools, for example, is a violation of separation of church and state. Therefore the Constitution (or the American tradition) forbids Federal or State aid to such schools."

In the following pages we shall examine the major and minor premises of this argument. The next four chapters will describe the historical progress of the First Amendment from its introduction in 1791 to the present day, in an effort to discover what true sense can be attributed to separation of church and state in our legal and constitutional tradition.

The three subsequent chapters will discuss the idea of separation as a principle and policy, attempting to arrive at a definition of it which will be ethically as well as legally satisfying. In this part, the objective will be to show that a workable principle can be formulated if we make the approach from the point of view of the American theory of the state, and not from some theory of the nature of the church, as has so often been done, with little hope of agreement, since the differences on that ground are theological.

In the three final chapters it will be necessary to examine and analyze the arguments that have been advanced against the position taken here, particularly in connection with the Supreme Court decisions on the New Jersey bus-fare case and the Champaign, Illinois, religious-teaching case.

This brief book has been written in the great hope that at least some of the confusions and obscurities that have fogged discussions of separation of church and state will be cleared away, and that this will lead to a new agreement of minds and hearts over a problem that is one of our most important at this time.

Chapter Two

The Constitution
1789

IN A speech before a department of the National Education Association at Atlantic City, Dr. F. Ernest Johnson, professor at Teachers College, Columbia University, said:

"To ignore the distinction in function between church and state would be disastrous both to religious and to political freedom. But to make of the doctrine a rule of thumb to be invoked against every measure that brings church and state into some cooperative relationship is to travesty an important principle and thus to make it more obscure."

In this same speech he remarked:

"The notion that there is an 'American way' in this matter of the relation of religion to public education is utterly false to the facts." [1]

[1] F. Ernest Johnson, "Religion and Public Education," *Proceedings* of the Thirty-first Annual Convention, Secondary School Principals (1947), pp. 96-97.

What, then, are the facts? Is there an "American tradition of separation of church and state"? And, if there is, in what sense should it be taken without making a travesty of it?

To leave aside for the moment the more extreme approaches to these questions, a legal and historical basis of an American tradition in this matter is usually sought principally in the First Amendment, but also in Article 6, Section 3, of the United States Constitution, and in the writings of Thomas Jefferson and James Madison.

The First Amendment reads, in part:

"Congress shall make no law respecting an establishment of religion or prohibiting the free exercise thereof."

And Article 6, Section 3:

"No religious test shall ever be required as a qualification to any office or public trust under the United States."

It is well known that, at the very beginning of the Revolution, Thomas Jefferson started a long campaign to disestablish the Church of England in his native state, Virginia.[2] The famous Virginia Bill of Rights adopted at the Williamsburg Convention of 1776 was not directly influenced by

[2] See Jefferson's own words in *The Complete Jefferson*, ed. by Saul K. Padover (1943), esp. pp. 1288, 518, 537, 538, 544.

him, it is true, since he was in Philadelphia at that historic moment, but he was in accord with the ideas of its principal author, George Mason, and he carried on where it left off. The Church of England in Virginia was naturally in a very parlous state there once hostilities had begun, but it had also left itself open to attack by its intransigent attitude to other sects in colonial times. It had been disestablished at the beginning of the war, but in 1784 joined with some Presbyterians to gain state financial subsidy for religious worship in the famous Assessment Bill, which had the powerful support of George Washington, Patrick Henry, Richard Henry Lee, and John Marshall.[3]

James Madison, who represented Jefferson, then in France, led the fight against the Bill, and it was beaten by three votes.[4] Madison interjected into this struggle his famous *Memorial and Remonstrance*, which is credited with turning the popular tide against the Bill. Madison, from his student days at Princeton, had been disgusted by the sectarian differences in Protestantism, and, when he returned to active life in his State, he became an

[3] Hamilton J. Eckenrode, *Separation of Church and State in Virginia* (1910), p. 83.
[4] Cf. *ibid.*, p. 113.

opponent of the dominant church.[5] It is his *Remonstrance*, issued in this political battle, which has been brought forward recently as an authentic interpretation of the First Amendment to the Constitution, which he was to introduce in the First Congress five years later. As a result of the defeat of the Assessment Bill, Madison reintroduced Jefferson's original bill for religious liberty. When amended to form a compromise between Patrick Henry's idea of toleration and George Mason's and Jefferson's idea of complete liberty, it was passed January 16, 1786, with the thought of complete liberty predominating.[6]

The constitutional provision against religious tests, according to Madison's notes, was accepted in the Convention almost without debate. On August 20, 1787, Charles Pinckney of South Carolina proposed it in one form; on August 30, in another. On that same day, after only three short speeches, it was adopted unanimously—"*nem. con.*," in Madison's phrase. It was slightly amended on September 12, and finally adopted on September 17, after the Committee on Style and Arrange-

[5] Gaillard Hunt, *Life of James Madison* (1902), esp. pp. 1-12.

[6] Hunt, *op. cit.*, p. 84; Sanford H. Cobb, *The Rise of Religious Liberty in America*, pp. 495-497.

17

ment had approved it.[7] It is the only mention of religion in the body of the Constitution.

There is little to enlighten us as to what the Convention had in mind when this happened. It may merely be noted here in passing that most of the States did have then, and for many years after —and have in some cases even now—religious tests for office. All that the Constitution did was to forbid such tests for offices in the Federal Government, in view of the rivalry between the sects then existing in the separate States. The Constitution, of course, did not forbid religious tests for office under the States. This was thoroughly understood at the time, both in theory and in practice.

Two of our great commentators on the Constitution, Joseph Story and Charles Warren, are agreed on the reasons for this almost complete silence in the Constitution itself about religion.[8] Their conclusions are succinctly summarized in the Appellees' Brief in the McCollum case:

[7] See Madison's Notes, arranged in Arthur Taylor Prescott, *Drafting the Federal Constitution* (1941), p. 740.

[8] Joseph Story, *Commentaries on the Constitution*, 5th ed. (1891), Vol. I, p. 459, sec. 622; Vol. II, p. 633, sec. 1879; Charles Warren, *The Making of the Constitution* (1928), pp. 425-426.

"Religion was not mentioned, *first*, because it was intended that the Federal Government should have no control over the subject [9] just as the document made no mention of education or intrastate commerce for the same reason: and, *second*, because the religious beliefs and practices of the people throughout the States, as well as the extent of the control exercised over religion by the States, were so diverse that it was wholly impractical to attempt any uniform system of relationship between religion and government." [10]

This brief goes on, with entire fidelity to the historical record, to say that the Convention did not wish to express "any disinterest in religion or its welfare, but rather spoke eloquently of the anxiety of the Framers to protect it, foster it, and preeminently, to leave it a local rather than a national matter." [11] An examination of the debates in the State conventions called to ratify the Constitution fully bears out this statement. Those who opposed the great document for various reasons were uneasy, on this particular provision, lest

[9] Jonathan Elliott, ed., *The Debates in the Several State Conventions on the Adoption of the Federal Constitution* (1836), Vol. III, pp. 204-205.
[10] *McCollum* v. *Board of Education*, Appellees' Brief, p. 31.
[11] *Ibid.*

Papists, Mohammedans, Jews, and atheists might hold office under the Federal Government. Its proponents pointed out that, in a Federal system, such liberty was necessary (in the face of a diversity of even Protestant sects), and that, in any case, local governments were always free from such restrictions as to religious tests, where they still had them. Even with these explanations and reservations, large minorities were registered against the ratification.[12]

The First Amendment and the circumstances surrounding its adoption give us more information on this score. This Amendment, it will be remembered, is now the first article in the so-called American Bill of Rights. When the Constitution was submitted to the thirteen States for adoption by a three-fourths vote, there was considerable opposition to it on the ground that it did not include a bill of rights in the traditional English sense of historical guarantees of immunity against arbitrary acts at the hands of government.

In the next-to-last paper of the *Federalist*,[13] Alexander Hamilton answered the "clamors" of those, particularly in New York and Virginia, who demanded a bill of rights in the Constitution. by

[12] Elliott's *Debates,* esp. Vols. II, III, IV.
[13] *The Federalist,* No. 84.

saying that such a bill not only would be unnecessary but might be dangerous in a Constitution like that of the United States. "The Constitution is itself a bill of rights," in the traditional Anglo-American sense. The Federal Government was to have no powers except those enumerated in the Constitution, and, since no powers were there given to abridge the rights of the press, of assembly, of association, and of religious liberty, then it followed that these rights were completely safeguarded in it. The clamors continued, nevertheless, particularly in Virginia, and as a consequence James Madison introduced several amendments explicitly safeguarding fundamental liberties. One of these liberties was freedom of conscience before the state.

Now, to understand the reason for the inclusion of the provision concerning religion, it is necessary to recall the history of religious establishments in the colonies and the resulting thirteen States.

Before the Revolution, ten colonies had established churches: the Church of England was established in New York, New Jersey, Maryland, Virginia, North and South Carolina, and Georgia; the Congregationalist Church in Massachusetts (including Maine), New Hampshire (including

21

Vermont), and Connecticut. There was no established church in Rhode Island, Pennsylvania, or Delaware, though even in these three some churches had privileges.

During the Revolution or shortly after, as was natural, five of those States which had an established Anglican Church disestablished it—New York, New Jersey, Virginia, North Carolina, and Georgia. Thus, at the time of the Constitutional Convention in 1787, five States—all of New England (except Rhode Island), Maryland, and South Carolina—had established churches, while eight did not. All of the States, however, had religious tests for office of varying degrees of extent and intensity: Jews, Catholics, Quakers, Unitarians, and atheists were severally excluded from office in one or more of the States. Thus, even in those States which had no established churches, Protestants of various kinds were privileged and protected by the Constitutions.[14] Thus there was no American tradition, or practice, or principle, of "separation" of church and state on this particular score among the Founding Fathers.

What, then, did the United States Constitution do, and why was it done?

What it did is clear. It forbade the Federal Gov-

[14] Carl Zollmann, *American Church Law* (1933), pp. 2-5.

ernment to establish any church, and it also forbade it to place any disabilities on any person by its laws as a Federal Government by reason of his religion. It was a charter of religious liberty, as far as the Federal Government was concerned. *It did not lay the same restraints upon the States.* This latter statement can be proved from every writer on the Constitution and from many Supreme Court decisions.

Their unanimous opinion is thus summed up by Charles A. Beard in his dialogue commentary on the Constitution:

"Before the Fourteenth Amendment was adopted in 1868, any State was constitutionally free to establish a church, impose religious tests on voters and office-holders, turn education over to parsons and priests, require everybody to attend church, and in fact to set up a religious monopoly about as strict as that which obtained in Western Europe during the Middle Ages. That is, as far as the Federal Constitution was concerned, a State could do all this." [15]

And Carl Zollmann says:

"The First Amendment is a restraint on the action of *Congress,* and is not a restriction on the action of the *State Legislatures.* 'The Constitution

[15] Charles A. Beard, *The Republic* (1943), p. 170.

makes no provision for protecting the citizens of the respective States in their religious liberties; this is left to the State constitutions and laws; nor is there any inhibition imposed by the Constitution of the United States in this respect on the States.' [16] Any action by a State establishing some religion and prohibiting the free exercise of all other religions would therefore not be in contravention of it." [17]

This is amply proved by the fact that Connecticut, for instance, did not disestablish its church until 1818, Massachusetts not until 1833, and New Hampshire by its Constitution to this day may legislate for "adequate provision . . . for the support and maintenance of public Protestant teachers of piety, religion and morality."

It is very clear, therefore, that there is no very long-standing general legal principle of separation of church and state in this country as that term is being used now. We have it on the words of Judge Joseph Story, the great early commentator on the Constitution, writing in 1833, that every American colony down to the Revolution, excepting possibly Rhode Island, "did openly by the whole course of its laws and institutions, support

[16] *Permoli* v. *First Municipality* (1845), 44 U.S. 589, 609.
[17] Zollmann, *op. cit.*, p. 8.

24

and sustain in some form the Christian religion, and almost invariably gave a peculiar sanction to some of its fundamental doctrines." [18]

That last statement was especially true of the States' action with regard to their public schools, and it was only after 1845 that these were made non-sectarian, and then only in a peculiar sense, as we shall see. Judge Story further said, in the same place, that "this has continued to be the case in some of the States down to the present period [1833] without the slightest suspicion that it was against the public law or republican liberties." It would be very strange if it were otherwise, since a very slight knowledge of our early history and of the writings of the time will show how deeply religious was all but a very small segment of the American population.[19]

From all this it follows that what really happened when the First Amendment was proposed was that the several States were demanding to keep to themselves the right of having an established

---

[18] Story, *Commentaries*, II, sec. 1873.

[19] Speaking of the Constitutional Convention, for example, Edwin C. Goddard says: "Every one of its members was a believer in God and in future reward and punishment, and most of them, including the presiding officer, Washington, were church members" (*Michigan Law Review*, 10:166).

church, if they so desired, and as some of them had at the time. The whole discussion revolved around the question of States' rights as against Federal rights.[20] This will become clearer if we examine the motives of those who introduced and voted for the First Amendment.

To do that we have to revert to the position of religion in the thirteen original States. As we have seen, they fell into four groups. The New England States, except Rhode Island, had established churches of the Congregationalist denomination. Two States—Maryland and South Carolina—had Episcopalian establishments. Five States—New York, New Jersey, Virginia, North Carolina, and Georgia—had only recently disestablished the Church of England, but still retained it in variously privileged positions. Three States—Rhode Island, Pennsylvania, and Delaware—had never had an established church.

With this situation in mind, then, it is easy to see that the only possible solution to be arrived at by the Congress was to accept an amendment to the Constitution (once it was decided to have an amendment) which would favor no one church

[20] William Haller, "The Puritan Background of the First Amendment," in *The Constitution Reconsidered*, ed. Conyers Read (1938), p. 134.

over another. If Congress were to be allowed to establish the Episcopalian Church, the Congregationalists obviously would be disgruntled; if the Congregationalists were favored, the Episcopalians would be affronted; while, if either had been taken, the Baptists in Rhode Island and the Quakers in Pennsylvania would demur. It is clear that the only possible outcome that political wisdom could dictate was to forbid the Federal Government to establish any church, to treat all churches on a basis of equality, and to allow each State to establish a church of its choice, or not, as it pleased.

When the Constitution was ratified by vote of three-fourths of the State Conventions, several of these felt that guarantees against religious discrimination by the Federal Government should have been included in the fundamental law. Accordingly, Virginia, New York, and North Carolina proposed amendments which were almost identical.[21] There was one clause which was common to all of these: it condemned discriminatory legislation in favor of one religion over all others. For instance, Madison brought with him Virginia's amendment: ". . . and no *particular* religious sect

[21] See, for Virginia and North Carolina respectively, Elliott's *Debates*, Vol. III, p. 659, and Vol. IV, p. 244.

or society ought to be favored or established by law *in preference to others.*" There was nothing in these proposed amendments forbidding *religion* to be favored by the Federal Government; there was only a prohibition against one *form* of religion being favored over all others. These State Conventions were thinking in terms of equality of all the sects before the Federal Government, and so, as we shall see, did the First Congress that adopted the First Amendment. If the Federal Government had any favors for religious groups, these were to be available to them all.

It was not, then, a doctrine or "principle" of separation of church and state that motivated those who proposed the First Amendment. It was a policy to be adopted. It was found that, unless the Federal Government were inhibited from establishing any church, it would be extremely difficult, if not impossible, to get the Constitution ratified by many States. If the people of a State could not have their church established nationally, they were not going to allow any other to be established.

James Madison, who had worked hard to get his State of Virginia to ratify the Constitution, was forced to pledge himself to work for an amendment forbidding Federal establishment,[22] though he agreed with Hamilton that no bill of rights should be in the Constitution. It was only on that pledge as given by him that Virginia ratified at all. New York also was afraid that one sect might be established by Congress, and took the same stand as Virginia. The First Amendment was the price that Madison and others paid to secure ratification of the Constitution. Thus, Zollmann speaks of "the practical impossibility of selecting a national state church from among the various denominations willing to be considered for the honor . . . all were unwilling to concede any favor by the Federal Government to any denomination but their own . . ."[23]

[22] *Writings of James Madison* (1865), Vol. I, p. 423; *Annals of Congress,* Vol. I (1789), p. 424.
[23] Zollmann, *op. cit.,* p. 8.

Chapter Three

The First Amendment

1791

JAMES MADISON, as leader of the House of Representatives, culled twelve out of the more than 200 amendments to the Constitution that had been presented in one way or another, and laid them before the House, sitting as a Committee of the Whole, on June 8, 1789. The amendment on religious liberty, at that time the fourth on his list, read:

"The civil rights of none shall be abridged on account of religious belief, nor shall any national religion be established, nor shall the full and equal rights of conscience in any manner or on any pretext be infringed." [1]

This is the *first version* of the First Amendment. As we shall see, it was to be greatly modified in the legislative process. As is clear, it consisted of

[1] *Annals of Congress*, Vol. I, p. 434.

three parts: (1) religious *beliefs* shall not be a liability as far as concerns *civil* rights, that is, rights before the state; (2) the Federal Government is forbidden to establish a *national* religion; (3) the rights of conscience (what a man believes before God to be just and true) are not subject to state dictation.

Even this first form, as delivered by Madison, is very far from the doctrine of Madison's own *Remonstrance* and the Virginia Legislature: that the state may not aid religion in any way or have anything to do with it. Madison did not believe, evidently, that he should bring Virginia's own difficulties with the Church of England into the national arena. It is clear, however, that there is here a theory of the state in regard to religion which is evolved out of what the state is conceived to be, not out of the nature of religion. The distinction is important, as we shall see.

It may be remarked in passing that, two days after Madison introduced this amendment before the House, Bishop John Carroll of Baltimore published in the *Gazette of the United States* his famous reply to the demands of a still unknown writer ("E. C.") in the same newspaper some weeks before (May 5, 1789) that the Protestant religion be made the established religion of the nation. In his reply, Bishop Carroll asserted "the great principle of religious freedom" and "the sacred rights of conscience" before the state. It is clear that the Catholic Church in the United States already was thinking of the state in the particular concrete form in which it was to evolve in America.[2]

All of Madison's amendments on civil rights were referred on July 21 to a select committee of one from each State, of which he himself was named the member from Virginia, and on July 28 this committee reported out the religious amendment to the House in the following abbreviated form:

"No religion shall be established by law, nor shall the equal rights of conscience be infringed." [3]

This is the *second version* of the Amendment. It is also the second reference in Congress to *establishing* religion. But the introduction of the word is significant. It showed what the Congress held paramount; namely, that the Federal Government as such should adopt no religion as the national religion, and that it would never be allowed to use the power of the state as such to force consciences to adopt any one religion.

[2] J. Moss Ives, *The Ark and the Dove* (1936), pp. 389 ff.
[3] *Annals,* Vol. I, p. 729.

It must be remembered that these men were producing for the world a kind of government which had no historical parallel for it. It was to have certain enumerated powers, granted to it by the people of the States, but no others among those which people had always agreed a state might have. It was commonly agreed that religion was not among these powers which the Federal State was to possess, whatever the individual States might have, which was not then in debate.[4]

In the course of the debate on the form of the amendment, as proposed by the committee, Daniel Carroll (brother of the bishop), who seems to have been delegated by Madison to bear the brunt of the argument, after four rather slight contributions by others, is thus reported:

"As the rights of conscience are, in their nature, of peculiar delicacy, and will little bear the gentlest touch of governmental hand; and as many sects have concurred in opinion that they are not well secured under the present Constitution, he said he was much in favor of adopting the words.

[4] Madison's Fifth Amendment was intended to be a limitation upon the States: "No State shall violate the equal rights of conscience, or the freedom of the press, or the trial by jury in criminal cases" (*Annals*, Vol. I, p. 435). This proposed amendment died in committee.

He thought it would tend more toward conciliating the minds of the people to the Government than almost any other amendment he had heard proposed." [5]

During the course of the debate of this day, however, while Congress was still sitting as Committee of the Whole, Congressman Samuel Livermore of New Hampshire presented a new form of the amendment:

"Congress shall make no laws touching religion, or infringing the rights of conscience." [6]

This all-inclusive proposal, the *third version* of the amendment, and quite in accord with New Hampshire's ideas about forbidding Congress to have anything at all to do with religion, even indirectly, was accepted by the Committee of the Whole that day, by a vote of 31 to 20, but of course it did not have the requisite two-thirds majority for an amendment, as required for final action. It never came up again, and so this third version was lost. What happened was that the Committee of the Whole referred this amendment, along with others, to another special committee for further consideration.

Perhaps the most significant of all the debates

[5] *Annals,* Vol. I, pp. 729-30.
[6] *Ibid.,* p. 731.

occurred during this discussion of the second version, in the speech of Madison himself, on August 15. It is to this speech, immediately following that of Daniel Carroll, that we must look for what Madison really had in mind in introducing what became the First Amendment. He said:

"Whether the words are necessary or not, he did not mean to say, but they had been required by some of the State Conventions, who seemed to entertain an opinion that the clause of the Constitution, and the laws made under it, which gave Congress power to make all laws necessary and proper to carry into execution the Constitution, enabled them to make laws of such a nature as might infringe the rights of conscience and *establish a national religion; to prevent these effects he presumed the amendment was intended, and he thought it as well expressed as the nature of language would admit.*" [7]

Moreover, during the debate, he made his position still clearer. In answer to one who feared that such an amendment might favor those who had no religion at all, he said:

"If the word 'national' was inserted before 'religion' it would satisfy the minds of honorable gentlemen. *He believed that the people feared that*

[7] *Ibid.*, p. 730. (Italics mine.)

one sect might obtain a pre-eminence, or two com-
bine together, and establish a religion to which they
would compel others to conform. He thought if
the word 'national' were introduced it would point
the amendment directly to the object it was intended to prevent." [8]

This is Madison speaking as the proponent of an
amendment to the Federal Constitution and as a
national statesman, and it is widely removed from
the speeches and writings he produced as a politi-
cian in Virginia seeking the disestablishment of a
particular church he had come to dislike. There
can be no doubt that he intended the amendment
in this form, which he defended, as a bulwark
against the establishment of a particular form of
religion which would be preferred by the Federal
Government to all others. Charles Carroll, and his
kinsmen, the brothers Daniel and John Carroll, no
doubt had the same mind about it.

On this most significant part of the whole debate
in the Congress on the adoption of the First
Amendment, in place of any further commentary,
let me quote here the trenchant words of the *Brief*
of the Appellees in the McCollum case:

"In the face of the representations . . . on the

[8] *Ibid.* (Italics mine.)

part of Mr. Madison, it is little short of remarkable that anyone can ascribe to Mr. Madison an intention that the First Amendment should be given a different meaning than he himself assigned it in such debate. Are we to brush aside the indisputable historical fact that when questioned by his legislative colleagues, Madison said he apprehended the meaning of its words to be: 'that Congress should not establish a religion, and enforce the legal observation of it by law, nor compel men to worship God in any manner contrary to their conscience'?

"Are we now, 160 years after the Amendment was explained by Madison, to examine his writings and speeches outside of the legislative chamber, and from them to seek to determine what was his own personal political philosophy as to the relationship of Church and State, and then, disregarding his words at the time of the framing of the Amendment, ascribe to the Amendment the meaning thus gleaned?

"The plain fact is that, whatever Mr. Madison's personal political or philosophical views were about the undesirability of conferring benefits and aids upon religion and religious education, he did not as a legislator attempt to write into the Amendment any prohibition against equal government aid to all religions." [9]

This comment, made before the Supreme Court of the United States, is obviously a deliberate understatement. A minority of the Court in the Everson (New Jersey) bus case attempted to show from Madison's private opinions what was the meaning of the First Amendment, all but ignoring, except in a reference in a footnote, what Madison himself had meant by the Amendment as he presented it and debated it as it was amended. Surely, here was the place to find what the Amendment meant, and what Madison meant by it.

The third version which was introduced during this debate was not the last word by any means, nor the last which throws light on what the First Congress meant by the First Amendment. When the special Committee reported on it to the House on August 5, Congressman Fisher Ames of Massachusetts, in the course of the debate, proposed still another form:

"Congress shall make no law establishing religion, or to prevent the free exercise thereof, or to infringe the rights of conscience." [10]

This *fourth version* of the Amendment went

[9] McCollum case, *loc. cit.*, p. 43.
[10] *Annals*, Vol. I, p. 766.

over on August 20 to the Senate, after being passed by the House as more in accord with its idea of the state-religious problem. It rejected Congressman Livermore's radical proposal, and reverted to Madison's idea of religious liberty. We do not have detailed records of the proceedings of the Senate, which in the first two sessions were secret, but we do know that it considered the House's Amendment on August 25 and again on September 9, and on this day, after an extremely short consideration, it reported out the religious part of the amendment (now the third) as follows:

"Congress shall make no laws establishing articles of faith or a mode of worship or prohibiting the free exercise of religion, etc." [11]

This was the *fifth version* of the Amendment. It "did nothing to the House version but indicate the Senate's desire that the amendment contain nothing antagonistic to religion and to make clear that Congress should not establish a national religion and enforce observance of it by law. This was simply the Senate's way of expressing the meaning of the House, as shown in the debates in

[11] See *Annals*, Vol. I, pp. 71 and 77; also *Senate Document*, September 9, 1789 (U. S. National Archives), and *Gazette of the United States*, September 3, 1789.

the House." [12] The reasons why the Senate had substituted the words "establishing articles of faith or a mode of worship" for the House's formula "establishing religion" are fairly obvious. They were quite within the whole scope of the debate since Madison's first version had been presented: on the one hand, the Federal Government must not be presented as hostile to religion, as several Congressmen had feared it would be; on the other hand, it must not be suspected as favoring one sect over another. Elbridge Gerry of Massachusetts had already suggested: "It would read better if it was, that no religious doctrine shall be established by law." [13]

This fifth version of the Amendment then went into conference between committees of the Senate and House. Charles Carroll of Carrollton was one of the three on the Senate committee. Out of this conference came the final, and *sixth version,* of the Amendment:

"Congress shall make no laws respecting an establishment of religion or prohibiting the free exercise thereof."

The House approved this language on September 24, and the Senate on September 25, 1789,

[12] McCollum case, p. 46.
[13] *Annals,* Vol. I, p. 730.

and it was in this form that the religious part of the First Amendment went to the States for ratification.[14]

It is abundantly clear from this authentic history of the adoption of the First Amendment on religious liberty that all that both branches had in mind to propose to the States for amendment was a limitation on the Federal Government against imposing a national religion on the States and using its power to enforce any specific profession of belief on any citizen. Beyond this, no historical scholar and no commentator on the Constitution is entitled to go. What was said by any citizen in any previous discussion is completely irrelevant to any discussion of the Amendment itself. After all, only Congress can know what it means by an amendment it submits to the States.

That the Congress itself intended nothing further is also clear from its own make-up. The standing of the parties in the House was: Federalists, 52; Anti-Federalists, 12; and in the Senate, Federalists, 20; Anti-Federalists, 0.[15] The Federalists held steadfastly to the proposition that religion and morality, especially as taught in the

---

[14] *Ibid.*, pp. 913 (for the House) and 88.

[15] Theodore W. Cousens, *Politics and Political Organizations in America* (1942), p. 94.

41

schools, were necessary to Republican government.

The final position of Congress is clear. The Federal Government was faced with a diversity of sects, and hence, in the interests of the "more perfect union" on a country-wide level, that Government could not possibly favor one more than another. If one of the States had a homogeneous religion, there was nothing to prevent it from establishing or otherwise favoring that sect, and as we have seen, *nothing did*. The Federal Government, on the other hand, had to remain neutral among them all, by the very nature of that Government. It achieved this neutrality by simply abstaining from any law regarding an establishment of any church, and at the same time safeguarding before it the liberty and equality of all religions.

Equality of all religions, as far as the Federal Government was concerned, was the objective aimed at, not separation primarily—though that followed. Separation as a doctrine or principle did not enter the picture of the First Amendment. It was a specific policy that was adopted, not a principle. It is true, of course, that there were some secularists in those early days to whom all cooperation of church and state was abhorrent, but there is no evidence that they influenced the Amendment. Joseph Story, who was close to the events, said on this subject:

"An attempt to level all religions, and to make it a matter of state policy to hold all in utter indifference would have created a universal disapprobation, if not universal indignation. . . . The real object of the Amendment was to exclude all rivalry among Christian sects, and to prevent any national ecclesiastical establishment which should give to a hierarchy the exclusive patronage of the national government." [16]

It has been argued that, if we wish to get at the real meaning of the religious clauses of the First Amendment, we must rely on Madison's *Remonstrance* and the Virginia Bill for Establishing Religious Freedom. This argument, however, is completely overturned by the unfriendly reception Virginia itself gave the Amendment when it came up for ratification by its Senate.

It is well known that Virginia did not ratify until December 30, 1791, by which time a sufficient number of other States had ratified to make the ten Amendments binding on all the States. But the reasons for Virginia's attitude have remained

[16] Story, *Commentaries*, Vol. II, secs. 1874, 1877.

a forgotten chapter in history until they were recently rediscovered. First, her two Senators in Congress, R. H. Lee and William Grayson, wrote apologetically to the Virginia House of Representatives explaining why the Amendments did not measure up to the expectations of their State or its own Bill of Rights.[17] Then, the eight State Senators of the majority which had postponed ratification put into the record the reasons for their action. In this remarkable document, they find the Amendment "totally inadequate" and "far short of what the people of Virginia wish and have asked." They found that

"The third Amendment [now the first] recommended by Congress does not prohibit the rights of conscience from being violated or infringed; and *although it goes to restrain Congress from passing laws establishing any national religion,* they might, notwithstanding, levy taxes to any amount for the support of religion or its preachers; and any particular denomination of Christians might be so favored and supported by the general government, as to give it a decided advantage over the others, and in the process of time render it

[17] *Daily Advertiser* (New York), January 2, 1790, quoted in McCollum case, p. 50.

44

powerful and dangerous as if it was established as the national religion of the country." [18]

The Virginia Legislature obviously did not think the First Amendment to the Federal Constitution meant to forbid any kind of support to religion, however wrong they may have been in interpreting its effect on the equality of such support. Virginia, in fact, turns out to be the strongest contemporary witness *against* any interpretation of the Amendment as forbidding support, instead of the true source of the modern contention that the Amendment does forbid it. Virginia was the first to repudiate any such construction, and explicitly rejected the idea that her own Bill of Religious Freedom was the inspiration of the First Amendment. As a matter of historic fact, the Amendment was the joint thought of all the States, as the foregoing legislative history of the six versions of Madison's original amendment amply proves.

One final historical point remains to be cleared up, and that is the real meaning of the phrase "establishment of religion" in the First Amendment. In the *Brief* of the Appellants in the McCollum

[18] *Daily Advertiser,* January 26, 1790, reprinting *Journal* of the Virginia Senate of December 12, 1789; see McCollum case, pp. 51 ff. (Italics mine.)

case, and in certain incidental observations *(obiter dicta)* in the Everson case, it is held that this phrase means any kind of connection of the state with religion generally. A careful bit of research in the *Brief* of the Appellee in the McCollum case shows conclusively that the phrase, as used in the First Congress, bears no such construction.

By examining the use of the phrase in the contemporary State Constitutions, in the debates of the State conventions called for ratification, in the everyday usage, and in the practice of both the legislative and executive branches of the Government, the conclusion is reached that

"There is a continuous and unbroken stream of illustrations which demonstrate that everyone— voters and Framers alike—knew at the time of the adoption of the Amendment that the words 'establishment of religion' meant a state or national church or religion established by law and receiving preferences from government not equally enjoyed by others, including most commonly tax support for its clergy and houses of worship." [19]

From that day to this, in fact, the established Church of England has been commonly known as "The Establishment." Thus, the current edition of the *Encyclopaedia Britannica* has this entry:

[19] McCollum case, p. 55.

46

"ESTABLISHMENT: a word applied to certain religious bodies in their relation to the state. . . . Establishment implies the existence of some definite and distinctive relation between the state and a religious society (or conceivably more than one) other than that which is shared in by other societies of the same general character. . . . In a word, establishment is of the nature of a monopoly."[20]

This is especially clear in the debates that took place in the State conventions called to ratify the Constitution itself. The word "establishment" occurs on many pages of Elliott's *Debates*, especially on those reporting the discussions in Virginia and North Carolina. It is always used in connection with the legal setting up of one form of religion as the sole religion of the state, to the exclusion of others. In fact, both of these States proposed in identical words as an amendment to the Constitution: ". . . and that no particular religious sect or society ought to be favored or established by law in preference to others."

There can be no historical doubt that, when the First Amendment was written, the phrase "a law respecting an establishment of religion" meant ab-

[20] See *Establishment, Encyclopaedia Britannica*, 14th ed., Vol. VIII, p. 726.

solutely nothing more than a legislative act granting a monopoly of state favors to one particular religion. It is vain to read into it a prohibition against the state either dealing with religion as such, or assisting all religions equally.[21]

From the legislative history of the First Amendment, then, the following conclusions do not seem to be debatable:

(1) The thought of Congress, after debating and changing Madison's first version of the Amendment, crystallized around two basic ideas: The national government should adopt no religion as the official one of the United States, and it should respect the freedom of the exercise of any religion.

(2) Nothing was done about what the individual States might do in this regard and it was understood that each State retained the right of establishing the religion of its choice, or of supporting any or all religions, as many of them did for many years thereafter.

(3) Nothing was said or implied in the legisla-

[21] Edward S. Corwin, *The Constitution and What It Means Today*, 6th ed. (1938), p. 140: "An 'establishment of religion' means a state church, such as for instance existed in Massachusetts for more than forty years after the adoption of the Constitution."

tive process to the effect that the religious amendment to the Constitution forbade the Federal Government to maintain relations with various forms of religion, or even support them, provided it acted with equality and impartiality.

(4) The so-called "American principle of separation of church and state" simply did not exist at the time of the adoption of the First Amendment, while the policy of co-operation of the state with religion was universal.

(5) The ruling motive behind the adoption of the First Amendment was partly political—the Constitution would not have been ratified unless it was understood that the Federal Government would not interfere with local arrangements about religion; and partly legal—the national state that was being set up (whatever the individual States might do) was granted no competence of deciding in matters of religion as such.

(6) The final solution arrived at by the Congress was that the Federal Government should respect equality among competing religious denominations, and also the right of each individual, as far as the Federal Government was concerned, to belong to the denomination of his choice.

Chapter Four

Separation in the States
1791-1869

AFTER the adoption of the Federal Constitution, the States began little by little, and this
well into the nineteenth century, to withdraw the
restrictions on religious liberty which had existed
in practically all their own Constitutions.

The First Article of the Northwest Ordinance
(1787) was passed by Congress for what are now
the States of Indiana, Illinois, Michigan, Wiscon-
sin, and Minnesota: "No person demeaning himself in a peaceable and orderly manner shall ever
be molested on account of his mode of worship
or religious sentiments, in said territories." [1] As
these States began to fashion their Constitutions,
the Federal provisions for religious liberty were included. Meanwhile, also, those of the original thirteen States that had established churches began to

[1] See Zollmann, *op. cit.*, p. 4.

break the tie: Connecticut not until 1818, Massachusetts not until 1833, when the Congregationalist churches had become largely Unitarian. They were, however, more reluctant to change the provisions regarding religious tests for public office, on the theory, says Zollmann, "then generally prevailing, that only those who profess some form of religion are fit to hold public office." [2] Zollmann thus lists the tests the States then had, including Vermont which was admitted in 1791:

"While the Maryland Constitution required of all officers 'a declaration of belief in the Christian religion,' while the Massachusetts Constitution required of high executive and legislative officers a belief in the Christian religion and a firm persuasion of its truth, the fundamental law of Georgia, New Hampshire, New Jersey, North Carolina and Vermont limited such belief to the Protestant religion and was designed to require a positive and affirmative test and not merely the negative qualification of not being a Roman Catholic. The Delaware, Pennsylvania, and Vermont Constitutions further required an acknowledgment that both the Old and New Testaments are given by Divine inspiration. The Constitutions of Pennsylvania and Vermont in addition exacted a confession of a

[2] *Ibid.*, p. 5.

belief 'in one God, the Creator and Governor of the Universe, the rewarder of the good and the punisher of the wicked,' while the Delaware fundamental law imposed a veritable confession of Trinitarian faith, professing 'faith in God the Father, and in Jesus Christ His only Son, and in the Holy Ghost, one God, blessed forevermore.' " [3]

It would take too long to recount here the steps by which many of the original States divested themselves of most of the provisions regarding tests. Most of the existing State Constitutions have simply had copied in them the text of Article 6, Section 3, of the Federal Constitution regarding tests, but it is to be remarked that the presently existing Constitutions of Arkansas, Maryland, Mississippi, North Carolina, Pennsylvania, South Carolina, Tennessee, and Texas still require the acknowledgment or lack of denial of the existence of God or of the Supreme Being as a test for some offices. Pennsylvania and Tennessee also require a belief in a future state of rewards and punishments.[4]

Of course, since the Cantwell case (1940),[5] when the Fourteenth Amendment was declared by the Supreme Court to have extended to the

[3] *Ibid.*
[4] *Ibid.*, p. 7.
[5] *Cantwell* v. *Connecticut,* 310 U.S. 290, at 303.

States the same prohibitions concerning legislation restricting religious liberty that exist in the Federal Constitution, these provisions would undoubtedly be declared unconstitutional if challenged. They stand now as a silent testimony of a historical fact, refuting the principle of separation of church and state in the sense used nowadays: that the States shall have no connection with religion. This sense was unknown in early days, except, as I have remarked, in the writings of some anti-ecclesiastical radicals. Even now, the First Amendment applies in the States only in the measure of the meaning that may be given it by the Supreme Court in its decisions.

Moreover, the close tie-up between the States and religion was even more pronounced in practice than it was in law. The States were constantly giving material benefits to churches in the form of land, tax exemptions, appropriations, legal privileges and encouragements of every kind. On the other side, the ministers of religion were often real political leaders: they suggested and pushed legislation of many kinds; they were vocal in elections; they generally considered themselves protectors of the American form of government, which was commonly accepted as having its foundations in Christian teaching and morality. Readers of Ray

Allen Billington's *The Protestant Crusade* or Gustavus Myers' *History of Bigotry* will see how large a part Protestant ministers played in public affairs.

The absence of a principle of separation of church and state in a broader sense can best be seen, perhaps, in a consideration of the growth of the public schools, a field where a new conflict has lately begun.[6]

There were three types of schools in the colonies, all of them church or private schools, in which religious instruction was regarded as the primary responsibility of the school to insure civic and private virtue. In colonies like Virginia, where the Church of England was dominant, it was the Established Church which had the function of providing educational facilities, though private resources also furnished some schools. The parochial-school type existed in Pennsylvania, and also in New Jersey, Delaware, and early New York, where the school was essentially a part of the church organization of Quakers, Presbyterians, Lutherans, Moravians, and the Dutch Reformed.

[6] For much of the historical material on the following pages I am indebted to Sister Raymond McLaughlin, O.S.B., Ph.D., *A History of State Legislation concerning Private and Elementary Schools in the United States, 1870-1945* (1946), pp. 1-30, and authorities there cited.

The third type existed generally in New England, of which Moehlman well says:

"The New England schools, in the early period, were just as religious as those of the middle colonies. . . . The early New England town was also a unified church organization and represented both the civil and religious government. . . . The state existed to serve the religious organization and may be described as a bibliocracy [sic]. Since the New England church and the New England state were, for all practical purposes, merely different aspects of a single unity, it seemed natural that the state should promulgate the first laws governing education."[7]

As is known, the bonds of church and state in New England gradually relaxed, the causes of which it is not necessary to go into here, the chief being the inner doctrinal breakdown of rigid Calvinism. The result was that the state remained in control of education. The process was gradual, almost unnoticed, and even at the time of the adoption of the Constitution, while the New England state made the laws, the clergy ran the schools.

The state of mind regarding the relation of religion and the school at the time is well illustrated

[7] Arthur B. Moehlman, *School Administration* (1940), p. 12.

in the celebrated Third Article of the Northwest Ordinance, adopted by the Congress in 1787: "Religion, morality, and knowledge being necessary to good government and the happiness of mankind, schools and the means of education shall be forever encouraged." Translating this into modern language, it means: "Schools are the means by which religion, morality and knowledge are imparted, and since these three are necessary for good government and mankind's happiness, the state has the duty of encouraging the erection and conduct of schools." When the Southwest Ordinance was drawn up in 1790, it contained the same provision.

It is amazing that some modern writers should consider this section of the famous Ordinance as a sort of charter of the public school as we now know it. It is only by ignoring the first word of the document that such a distortion can be managed; and it may be noticed that the state is given the function of "encouraging" schools, not of conducting them. It would have been altogether out of character for the men of that time either to imagine that schools could be conducted without religion, or even, for the most part, that the state should do more than "encourage" the formation and conduct of schools.

It is true that there was about this time a considerable growth of secularism. Both Hamilton and Washington were greatly alarmed at this development, and that is no doubt why they put in the Farewell Address these famous words:

"Of all the dispositions and habits which lead to political prosperity, religion and morality are indispensable supports. . . . And let us with caution indulge the supposition that morality can be maintained without religion. Whatever may be conceded to the influence of refined education on minds of peculiar structure, reason and experience both forbid us to expect that national morality can prevail in exclusion of religious principle. It is substantially true that virtue or morality is a necessary spring of popular government. . . . Promote, then, as an object of primary importance institutions for the general diffusion of knowledge."

There is here the same assumption that religion and morality are a necessary adjunct of education that is seen in the Northwest Ordinance. In 1796, as in 1787, there was no separation of church and state in the modern sense, as far as the schools are concerned. And it is also significant that the state is to "promote" education, not conduct it, just as the Ordinance prescribed that schools should be "encouraged." It was not considered to be within the scope of government to teach. The modern trend toward governmental control of schools was as foreign to the mind of the men who made the Constitution as was the modern concept of separation of church and state. A totalitarian government has something to teach, and hence must control and dictate. A democratic government has fulfilled its function when it promotes and encourages good schools to turn out good citizens. It was not considered inconsistent with the function of education in a democracy for the government to grant funds, which it has the right to raise by taxes, to schools controlled and operated by churches.

Yet, in the course of time, a separation came about, and the causes of this development must now be examined.

There were no immediate changes in educational attitudes and practices with the coming of national independence. The churches and the private agencies continued to provide the money, the teachers, and the curricula for the schools, in which the religious purpose continued to be dominant. There were also many cases where the public authority came to the support of their private efforts. Some few common schools supported by public taxes were established.

By the turn of the century, many of the inner difficulties that plagued the States in their beginnings had been ironed out. These had kept them from devoting much attention to the schools, which were left to the churches to run. But, with the growth of popular democracy around 1800, the increasing diversity of religious sects, the decline of religion itself as a motive force in private and public life, and the growing population, which made support of private schools a burden, the legislatures began to turn their eyes more and more to the schools.

These conclusions began to emerge: (1) The promoting of universal popular education became an urgent need in a democracy; (2) The multiplying sects in each State made it inadvisable to choose between them; (3) The job of running schools was beginning to be too big for many churches which were losing their congregations; (4) Popular opposition to church control of all the schools was a hard nut for the politicians to crack. The policy began to crystallize. In 1818, Connecticut, the first to do it, put into its Constitution this provision: ". . . no law shall ever be made authorizing such [school] funds to be devoted to any other use than the encouragement and support of public or common schools among the several school-societies, as justice and equity shall require." So far as I know, this is the first time that the term "public school" is used to denominate a school not under church auspices. The term "common school" had come into use for some time. The school societies, however, were a new development. They were a secular competitor of the church school—secular, but not necessarily governmental, though now in Connecticut government-supported, and exclusively so. Soon, as in New York, they were to be taken over by the State entirely.

Nevertheless, even by the 1820s there was no perceptible indication that the earlier conviction of the importance of religion in the schools had been abandoned. Many of the church schools had been absorbed into the publicly supported common schools, yet teachers, textbooks, curricula, and religious instruction were still to continue in them unchanged for many years. There are many instances of state support by taxes or by authorized lotteries for private, or church, schools. In other words, up to nearly fifty years after we are told that the First Amendment had introduced separation of state and church in the schools, there is little evidence of it in history.

The irreligious and the secularists were, however, becoming increasingly vocal in American life, particularly in education. A part of their influence stemmed from the influx of French Revolutionary ideas, which were atheist and secularist in the extreme, part of it from an admiration for the new Prussian school system, which seemed to Americans to embody the rampant nationalism of the times.

Some educational historians are inclined to attribute to the Prussians a great influence on the development which American education was shortly to take, as if the Prussians were as secularist as these historians would like to think them to be. The fact is, however, that the Prussian system was administered in different localities on the parity principle as purely denominational schools. Our American school authorities seem to have ignored this point, and for the next fifty years a great period of transition set in, in which state systems of free, compulsory, tax-supported, state-controlled public schools became the type that dominated, and the early private and Protestant church schools began to decline and even to disappear. It is an ironical, and instructive, fact that it was precisely at this period that the Catholic parochial school began to make its appearance. The

Catholics were beginning where the Protestants left off.

In the late 1830s, Horace Mann, Secretary of the Massachusetts State Board of Education, appeared as a portent in the cause of public education. Mann, of course, is generally considered the father of the public school in the United States. He was a Unitarian, and probably a secularist himself, influenced both by the French Revolution in one sense, and by his idea of the Prussian system in another. But his immediate practical aim was different from both. He came in the middle of an evolution of thought tending to look more and more on education as a function to be carried out, not merely "encouraged," by the democratic state. From this, it was a facile transition to the conclusion that the state's schools could not favor one religion more than another. That in turn led to another conclusion, namely, that the state schools should be non-sectarian, and that "sectarian" schools should be denied any state funds. As Secretary of the State Board of Education (1837-1848), he proceeded to put these conclusions into execution. Whatever the whole complex of motives was that led to this development (and anti-religion entered into it to a certain extent), the example of Massachusetts was widely copied. Between 1837 and 1875, fourteen State Constitutions were amended to forbid State funds for non-public schools.

It must not be imagined, however, that the public school as it left the hands of Horace Mann, Henry Barnard, Thaddeus Stevens, Samuel Lewis, Samuel Galloway, and the other associates in this movement, was the same in regard to religion as the public school is today. "Non-sectarian" did not mean "without religion," still less "irreligious." It meant what it said: it was religious, but was controlled by no sect—Baptist, Congregationalist, Lutheran, Anglican. A "sectarian" school was one controlled by a "sect," including, obviously, the Catholic Church.

The price the Protestants paid for giving up their own sectarian schools was not giving up religion in the schools. They retained the Protestant religion, but in the schools, as distinct from the churches, it was a Protestantism of no particular sect, hence, "non-sectarian." "Thus," as a recent writer remarks, " 'non-sectarian' religion (*i.e.*, that which did not discriminate among the creeds of the various Protestant sects) was regarded as entitled to public support, while those who adhered to 'sectarian' religion (*i.e.*, the Catholic creed) were not entitled to it." [8]

Thus, the situation was at the beginning really not much different from what it was before. Religion was still in the public schools, but it was no longer Methodist or Baptist religion; it was "nonsectarian religion." With the growth of various sects everywhere, it had simply become impossible to decide which religion should be taught in the schools, and, as a practical solution, it was agreed that no specific one should be taught, provided it remained non-Catholic Christianity.

The Protestant ministers who acquiesced in this measure of religious peace did not imagine they were giving up religion in the schools. It would have been against the whole general spirit of the age if they had. As a matter of fact, also, in many communities, where one sect was dominant, the tinge of religious influence in the public school was that of the local pastor; the school was usually built next to the Protestant church; assemblies and commencements were held there and were addressed by the pastor. This occurred even in the late nineteenth century in such a large city as

[8] Jerome Hannan, "The New Jersey Statute and the Supreme Court Minority," *American Ecclesiastical Review*, 116 (May, 1947), 336.

Philadelphia, and in many places the practice continues to this day. That may be one reason why many Protestant ministers still indignantly deny that the public school is "irreligious," or claim that, if it is, it is the protests of Jews and Catholics that have made it so.

In most larger cities, however, from the beginning there was an ironical result of the "non-sectarian" solution. Religion in the public schools became practically indistinguishable from Unitarianism; in other words, it was "sectarian" again. This was a common complaint from orthodox Protestant quarters. Meanwhile, in the place of origin of the non-sectarian public school, Massachusetts, trouble was brewing.

"The 'non-sectarianism' which Mann had succeeded in getting into the public schools was still definitely Protestant-tinged. The Catholic population was rapidly growing; difficulties existed in the way of establishing an adequate number of parochial schools. Nativism and Know-Nothing activities were breeding fear, hatred and riots." [9] There was some success in eradicating traces of Unitarianism and deism from the public schools, to satisfy orthodox Protestant scruples, and the reading of the Protestant Bible became quite gen-

[9] McLaughlin, *op. cit.*, p. 17.

eral (and it must be remembered that the reading of the Bible is for most Evangelicals their principal act of worship, with a quasi-sacramental character).

When this happened, says a Protestant writer, "and when the Roman Catholics appeared in numbers sufficient to demand, with some possibility of success, that they be not subjected to what they considered a sectarian Protestant religious education, and that in lieu of that they be given money for parochial schools for the teaching of Catholic doctrines, a rising tide of Nationalism united the Protestant sects to provide in the fundamental law against a possible use of state money intended for common schools, in sectarian schools which were not in the regularly administered system of common schools. But it was more a matter of expediency than principle, *for care was taken to exclude colleges from the prohibition.*" [10]

The colleges, of course, were practically all conducted by the Protestant churches at that time, which clearly shows that the issue was not decided on any general principle of separation of church and state. The Massachusetts Know-Nothing Legislature of 1855 proposed such an Amendment to

[10] Sherman M. Smith, *The Relation of the State to Religious Education in Massachusetts* (1926), p. 211. (Italics mine.)

66

the Constitution of 1780, and the people ratified it immediately. And once again, this time in a welter of Nativism and Know-Nothingism, most of the States followed the example of Massachusetts.

The result of all this is well known. Gradually, but inexorably, "non-sectarian" lost its original meaning, and now meant "non-religious," "with no religion at all"; "sectarian" meant having any kind of religion. The result became that, where state money could not be given to sectarian schools, no religion of any kind could exist in tax-supported schools. The "non-sectarian" public school now meant a non-religious school. Sincere Protestants must have seen with increasing despair their hold on the public schools slipping away; to-day it is practically gone. And the secularizing unbelievers pushed with unrelenting vigor to strip away every vestige of religion from the public schools. Separation of church and the public school now at last meant separation of the school from religion. Separation of church and state gradually took on the same meaning, largely, no doubt, because of the influence of the struggle over the schools.

From the facts as set forth here, these conclusions are clear:

(1) The original reason for setting up a "non-sectarian" public school was a prudential one, seeking to conciliate the conflicting claims of the competing sects.

(2) "Non-sectarian" did not at first mean "non-religious"; far from it; it meant religious, but not of any specific *sect,* at least officially.

(3) Separation of church and state, as a principle, did not enter as a consideration into the process of setting up the public schools under the state; quite the contrary.

(4) The refusal to grant any public money for the "sectarian" schools did not arise from any similar consideration, but from the desire to safeguard the public schools as they were, under general Protestant auspices.

(5) In general, separation of church and state during this period still remained a very vague and seldom heard concept, as far as the States were concerned.

Chapter Five

Religious Liberty

1869 to the present

A S WE have seen, all the States had disestablished their church by the early nineteenth century. Not very many of them prohibit in their Constitutions an establishment of religion in the actual words of the Federal Constitution; only Iowa, South Carolina, and Utah copy the provision literally, as do substantially Alabama, Louisiana, and New Jersey.[1] Only one State forbids a "union of church and state" in so many words, and that, ironically enough, is Utah, where it has often been difficult to see where the Mormon Church leaves off and the State begins. The formula, "separation of church and state," appears nowhere, and, as we have seen, it was not specifically in the minds of people, especially of Protestant believers. The emphasis in the Constitutions

[1] Zollmann, *op. cit.*, p. 18.

of the States is rather on religious liberty of the individual and equality of the churches, and this is expressed in many various ways, listed by Zollmann,[2] who is able to conclude: "Taking these provisions of the State and Federal Constitutions together it is clear that the American citizen enjoys the fullest protection of his religious liberty which human ingenuity can devise." At the same time, it is clear that separation of church and state and religious liberty are not the same thing. England, for example, has union of church and state, yet has had religious liberty since Catholic Emancipation in 1829.

We have also seen what motives and circumstances brought about in the State Constitutions the prohibition of granting State funds to "sectarian" institutions, acceded to by Protestants under the original understanding that a "non-sectarian" institution was not one which excluded religion from within it. The same prohibition as to funds for sectarian institutions was not, until very recent times, considered to be anywhere in the Federal Constitution. The proof of this is found in the fact that from the time of President Grant in 1875, to 1947, beginning with the Blaine Amendment, there have been no less than twenty-

[2] *Ibid.*, pp. 18-21.

one resolutions offered in Congress to amend the Federal Constitution so as to forbid the use of Federal funds for sectarian purposes. *If it had been thought that the Federal Constitution did forbid such grants, it is obvious that it would not be necessary to amend it.* In the Everson and McCollum cases, it was argued that the Supreme Court should now lay upon the States, by virtue of the Federal Constitution, a restraint which up to very recent years was not considered to be in the Constitution at all and which, when it was proposed to Congress, had consistently been rejected by it.

The new argument is that the Fourteenth Amendment to the Constitution (adopted in 1868) extends the provisions of the First Amendment to the States, that what this Amendment forbade to the Federal Government is now forbidden to the States as well. Let us examine this argument.

The Fourteenth Amendment reads in part:

"No State shall make or enforce any law which shall abridge the privileges or immunities of citizens of the United States, nor shall any State deprive any person of life, liberty or property without due process of law; nor deny to any person within its jurisdiction the equal protection of the law."

It is true that, since 1931, a series of Supreme Court decisions has held that certain guarantees of the First Amendment are by implication an integral part of the due-process clause of the Fourteenth Amendment, and that, consequently, these provisions of the First are now applicable to the States through the Fourteenth Amendment.[3] These provisions are: freedom of speech (*Stromberg* v. *California,* 1931); freedom of the press (*Lovell* v. *City of Griffin,* 1938); freedom of assembly (*DeJonge* v. *Oregon,* 1937); and the free-exercise-of-religion clause (*Cantwell* v. *Connecticut,* 1940). Until the Everson case (1947), however, no attempt was made to include the establishment-of-religion clause also under the same doctrine. In that case, both the decision of Justice Black and the dissent of Justice Rutledge essayed to take this further step. In his decision, Justice Black's remarks fall under the category of *obiter dicta,* and hence are not an essential part of the decision itself. In the McCollum case, involving released time for religious teaching in public schools, the Court was asked by the Appellant to

[3] For legal information on this and following pages, I am indebted to Francis J. Powers, C.S.V., *Religious Liberty and the Police Power of the State* (1948), chs. 3, 5.

make official the inclusion of the establishment-of-religion clause under the Fourteenth Amendment.

In this latter case, however, the Appellee clearly showed by constitutional doctrine and by Court precedents that the establishment-of-religion clause does not square with the other provisions of the First Amendment. This clause, unlike the others, was adopted for the purpose of dividing power as between the Federal and State Governments, as has been shown in earlier chapters. It merely sought to restrain the Federal Government from operating in the field of "establishment of religion." It did not involve personal rights as such, as the other clauses do, but divided the powers of Federal and State Governments respectively. The Courts have consistently refused to extend provisions intended to be restraints on the use of Federal power to the States as well, where the intent was merely to divide powers.

Hence:

"The establishment-of-religion clause comes within that class of Amendments having a meaning peculiar to the Federal Government; . . . at the time of its adoption it referred to the subject matter of an 'establishment of religion' in a National sense only, and . . . such inherent meaning has not changed, so that the clause is still limited to the Federal Government." [4]

In his decision in the Everson case, Justice Black essayed to give a list of what the establishment-of-religion clause forbids. Among these were the following:

"Neither [a State nor the Federal Government] can pass laws which aid one religion, or all religions, or prefer one religion over another; . . .

"No tax, in any amount, large or small, can be levied to support any religious activities or institutions, whatever they may be called, or whatever form they may adopt to teach or practice religion."

At the end of this passage, Justice Black gives the citation: "*Reynolds* v. *United States*, 98 U. S. 145, 164." An examination of this case, however, reveals the fact that this decision does not contain the items listed above, and Mr. Black does not allege any other precedents. There is, in fact, no prior decision which extends the establishment-of-religion clause to the States; still less, any which would forbid either the Federal or the State Governments to apply tax-raised money to religious purposes, by virtue of the First through the Fourteenth Amendment.

[4] McCollum case, p. 116.

Moreover, these *obita dicta* of Justice Black about separation of church and state cannot be properly evaluated without taking into consideration the words he used almost immediately afterwards about the First Amendment.[5] He remarked that this Amendment does not prohibit a State from spending tax-raised funds "as a part of a general program." Later, after mentioning some public services which every parochial school receives, he added these decisive words:

"Of course, cutting off church schools from these services so separate and so *indisputably marked off from the religious function,* would make it far more difficult for the schools to operate. But such is obviously not the purpose of the First Amendment. That Amendment requires the state to be a neutral in its relations with groups of religious believers and non-believers; it does not require the state to be their adversary. State power is no more to be used to handicap religions, than it is to favor them."[6]

[5] Since the above was written, Justice Black has denied that these words were *obiter dicta,* declaring that they form part of the official interpretation of the Court. But see below, Chapter 11.

[6] Supreme Court of the U. S., No. 52, October Term, 1946. Edition of the New York Catholic Welfare Committee (1947), pp. 12-15. (Italics mine.)

During the past ten years, several religious-liberty cases have come before the Supreme Court which have created developments highly important in the matter we have been discussing. These cases, however, were brought and decided under the religious-liberty clause. Most of these arose out of local legislation directed against the activities of the Jehovah's Witnesses. New doctrines have emerged; new precedents have been created. We have already mentioned the extension of the First Amendment to the States by a new interpretation of the Fourteenth Amendment not foreseen or intended by its makers when that Amendment was adopted in 1868. Then, there is the dispute in the present Court between the conflicting theories of Court action: the one called "political process," the other "more exacting judicial scrutiny." The former, held by Justice Frankfurter, would forbid the Court to overturn State legislation, even if against religious liberty, if there still exists in the State the political process by which the aggrieved party can agitate to reverse the legislation, from which it would logically follow that a majority in any State is supreme, and can do anything it pleases, provided a democratic form of government there still exists.

Justice Stone, in his famous one-man dissent in

the Gobitis case, opposed to this theory what he called "a more exacting judicial scrutiny." What he meant by this is that there are certain fundamental rights which even the States are bound to respect, and that it is the duty of the Supreme Court to protect these rights against any legislative majority.

This dispute, in turn, brought into action another judicial principle, that of the so-called "preferred rights." Not every civil right, according to this principle, should be invariably protected by the Court against the States, but the "preferred rights" certainly should. These are the rights of freedom of speech, of the press, of assembly, and of conscience. It is this principle which has ruled most of the recent majority decisions of the Court, though Justice Frankfurter has not consistently been willing to include freedom of religion within the preferred rights.

Finally, a fourth principle had also been active in the Court's decisions concerning religious liberty, a principle which goes by the name of "clear and present danger." This is a test for measuring the validity of legislation in the domain of religious liberty and freedom of expression. It is assumed that even religious liberty is not an absolute right without any limits. There are certain other paramount interests which the State must protect, and they may not be endangered under the false disguise of religion. However, following Justice Holmes, the Court now holds that there must be a "clear and present danger" to these interests before it will uphold State legislation restricting any of the preferred rights. The converse of this is also true, of course; namely, that when there is a clear and present danger to paramount interests the Court will uphold restrictive legislation. And this, joined to Justice Frankfurter's doctrine of "political process," could some day prove rather disastrous to religious liberty, if the Court should swing that way. However, the clear-and-present-danger standard, as presently interpreted to justify the restriction of only "the gravest abuses, endangering paramount interests," affords an extremely wide degree of protection to freedom of religion and expression. The freedom of the Jehovah's Witnesses to abuse Catholics and defy authority is an eloquent proof of the Court's determination to uphold religious freedom.

We have, then, these four developments:

(1) the same restriction as on the Federal Government laid on the States as regards the free exercise of religion;

(2) the more exacting judicial scrutiny of majority votes in the States;

(3) the listing of religion among the four preferred rights; and

(4) the clear-and-present-danger standard of whether State legislation is valid as concerns these rights.

What is important to note is that all these developments concern the exercise of *religion* and freedom of expression. If we exclude Justice Frankfurter's use of the doctrine of political process, and his inconsistency in refusing always to include freedom of religion among the preferred rights, they are not contrary to the historical meaning of the First Amendment's double injunction: prohibition of a preferred position to any one religion, to the disadvantage of the others; and equality of all religions before the state. This double injunction was designed to protect the liberty before the state of all those who profess a religion, and to guarantee equality of treatment in the exercise of this religion. As for those who profess no religion, or who repudiate religion, it is difficult to conceive how they can appeal to the First Amendment, since this document was solely concerned with religion itself, not its denial. By its very nature, as regards what it says about religion, they are outside its ken.

Chapter Six

Distinction and Co-operation

W E HAVE now to turn from the historical and constitutional aspects of this question to an examination of the concepts themselves which form the threads that run through the whole discussion: separation, distinction, co-operation—as regards church and state—religious liberty and equality.

First, however, let us examine the phrase "separation of church and state" in itself and see what it means.

It obviously does not mean what it says.

The state is a natural society which is devoted to temporal ends, the pursuit of temporal happiness, the good life. The church is a supernatural society which is devoted to spiritual ends, the pursuit of spiritual happiness, the eternal life. To bring about a true separation of these two societies is obviously impossible, unless you are going to tear each of the members physically into two pieces, *for the same people compose the two societies simultaneously.* You cannot even separate the two societies by placing the members of the church over here and the members of the state over there, for each of the people in one set would still continue to belong to the other set.

On the face of it, therefore, the phrase does not mean anything at all, and because it does not mean anything, it can be made to mean everything anybody wants it to mean, according to the exigencies of his argument. And that is precisely what has happened to it, even in the Supreme Court. It will be the task of this and succeeding chapters, therefore, to see whether there is any reality behind the clumsy and phantom phrase and how it operates in this country.

The phrase had a meaning in the minds of the European Masonic forces who seem to have been the first to use it in modern times against the Catholic Church. For them it meant an active unilateral process of separating the state from the church to which it had been attached for centuries by a strict juridical bond obligating both sides, for example, through a Concordat, as in France. It was this act of separating what had previously been juridically united that really deserved the name of separation. Later, the word was applied to the *result* of the act of separation, to designate a condition in which the two that had been partners were partners no longer. In this country, on the national level, no church was ever "united" with the Federal Government, as one or other had been in ten of the original thirteen colonies. The purely negative or static sense of separation of two that once had been united hardly applied over here. That is why the attempts to make it apply here have been so clumsy and the source of innumerable confusions.

Yet, it is obvious to everyone that in the United States the state and the church now exist in separate spheres, and, as far as the national Government is concerned, have always so existed. Every American has accepted that condition as the best possible political arrangement, and Catholics have not been backward in expressing their agreement with the national sentiment. As we have seen, Charles Carroll and the brothers, Daniel and Bishop John Carroll, were active in the fight to adopt the First Amendment. As late as January, 1948, another member of the Catholic hierarchy, Archbishop McNicholas of Cincinnati, Chairman of the Administrative Board of the National Catholic

Welfare Conference, expressed allegiance to our political and religious agreements in the following unequivocal terms:

"No group in America is seeking union of church and state; and least of all are Catholics. We deny absolutely and without any qualification that the Catholic Bishops of the United States are seeking a union of church and state by any endeavors whatsoever, either proximate or remote. If tomorrow Catholics constituted a majority in our country, they would not seek a union of church and state. They would then, as now, uphold the Constitution and all its Amendments, recognizing the moral obligation imposed on all Catholics to observe and defend the Constitution and its Amendments."

It is now time to examine the historical grounds on which Catholics have been able to join in this agreement, and the extent to which they will be able to join in a genuine American sense of separation.

The dualism of church and state as two distinct entities has its roots in the Gospels themselves. On a celebrated occasion, Jesus Christ said, in an answer to the taunts of His enemies attempting to make Him an enemy to the state: "Render to Caesar the things that are Caesar's, and to God the things that are God's." [1] The early Fathers of the Church saw it there in a nutshell. Before Christ, there was no distinction between religious and political functions: the priest was king and the king was priest in India, Egypt, Persia, Greece, Rome, and even to a great extent in Judah.

The great Christian Revolution, as far as this world was concerned, consisted in this, that hereafter Jesus Christ was setting up a new society alongside the state which He called the Church (fully equipped with appropriate organs: ruler, laws, executive, legislative and judiciary powers) and that hereafter the functions of those two societies should be considered distinct from each other. For centuries, the great struggle of the Church was, to put it in a perhaps startling phrase, to secularize the state; that is, to bring it about that the prerogative of power of the state did not extend to supernatural religion, but that the state nevertheless should have full rights in its own sphere, on the basis of natural law for the realization of the temporal happiness of man.

Since that time, we can see three great epochs in the relations of the Church with the temporal power: under the old Roman Empire, the medieval synthesis, modern times. In all of these we can dis-

[1] Matt. 22:21.

84

cern the operation of a pendulum, swinging now this way, and now that.

The first epoch, from the foundation of the Church to the final dissolution of the old Roman Empire, falls naturally into two parts: the first, up to the Edict of Toleration of Constantine in A.D. 313, when it was very clear that the two societies, state and church, were really distinct; the second, after that historic event, when the Emperors became Christian, but constantly attempted to treat the Church as merely a department of state, and dictated to it in every way. It was during the second part of this first epoch that a Pope, St. Gelasius (d. 496), set forth in unmistakable terms the historic doctrine of the Church. After pointing out that in ancient times the priest was king, and the king was priest, he reminds us that Christ came, and He was both Priest and King. When He left us, however, He did not wish that the two powers should remain in the hands of one man, and so He separated them.

"He divided the functions of each, assigning to each its proper task and dignity. . . . The spiritual power remains far removed from the temptations of the world, and, campaigning for God, does not mix into the affairs of the world, while on its side the secular power takes care not to undertake the direction of Divine things. By each one resting modestly in his place, each power avoids the pride of seizing absolute power, and thus holds a greater competence in the things that are his own." [2]

One of the immediate successors of Gelasius, Pope Symmachus, writing to a usurping and tyrannical Byzantine Emperor, and mindful of St. Paul's doctrine [3] that all power, temporal and spiritual, comes from God, said: "Do you obey God in me and I will obey God in you," [4] thus underlining the truth that each of the two powers is subject to the other in the things that are its own, whether God's or Caesar's, for both powers come from God.

This is the so-called Gelasian formula of the distinction between church and state, which has

[2] *Tractatus de Anathematis Vinculo*, Theil ed. (1868), Vol. I, p. 568. It was in a letter to the Emperor Anastasius that the same Pope wrote the famous passage beginning: "There are two, August Emperor, by whom the world is chiefly ruled, the sacred authority of the Pontiffs and the royal power" (p. 350).

[3] Romans 13:1: "Let every soul be subject to the higher powers, for there is no power but from God, and those that are, are ordained of God."

[4] Letter *contra Anastasium*, in *Migne, Patrologia Latina*, Vol. 62, col. 68.

86

remained the fundamental doctrine of the Catholic Church. Not every Emperor, or every Pope, obeyed its injunctions, but in our times Pope Leo XIII recalled it more forcibly to our minds and it is the official doctrine of the Catholic Church.

The second great epoch begins in the ninth century when Charlemagne first set up the Holy Roman Empire and lasts almost to modern times. During this period the picture changes. Where Gelasius saw two societies—with different ends and using different means—with two heads each operating in his own sphere, those of the Middle Ages saw one single society, the Christian people—with the identical end, the salvation of man, but using different means, spiritual or temporal, internal or external—and two heads, Pope and Emperor. There were two jurisdictions within Christendom, ecclesiastical and civil. There was no real distinction of church and state, as two societies. What we call church and state were then only two aspects of the same entity, the *populus Christianus*, Christendom.[5]

At a time when political unity was actually based on religious unity, the theory was clear. In practice, however, when the Pope was strong and the

[5] See R. W. & A. J. Carlyle, *Medieval Political Theory in the West*, 6v. (1930-1936), Vol. V, pp. 454-455.

Emperor weak, the Pope had the upper hand; when the Pope was weak and the Emperor strong, it was the Emperor who really ruled; but when both Pope and Emperor were strong, there was bitter clash, as between Gregory VII and Henry IV, or between Alexander III and Barbarossa. This ideal of political-ecclesiastical unity was still strong in people's minds well into modern times, even in Calvinistic and Anglican America. Even Catholic historians differ as to its real value.

The third epoch was marked by the rise of the national states, the breakup of Christian unity at the Reformation, and the spread of absolutism. In the thirteenth century, St. Thomas Aquinas had already found in Aristotle the philosophical foundation of the state as we know it today. He said that it is a "perfect" society, just as the Church is one also; that is, each fully contains within itself the means to fulfill its own distinct end. The state's end is the pursuit of temporal happiness; the Church's, the pursuit of eternal happiness; the state a natural society; the Church, a supernatural one. Each had its own sphere in which it operated.[6] The state, however, had its foundation

[6] St. Thomas Aquinas, Commentary on Aristotle's *Politics*, Lib. I, lect. 1; *Summa Theologica*, I-II, 90, iii ad 3; I, 96, iv in c; *In Lib. Sent.* II, dist. xliv, q. 2 ad 4.

in reason and the natural law of God; the Church, in the will of its Founder, Christ. Thus, each society was different from the other within the same nation, and so all the people could belong to each and owe allegiance to each under different aspects. St. Thomas was the first to define the state as a natural society.

But here again the pendulum swung from one side to the other. There was, it is true, new clarity on the older Gelasian formula of two distinct societies, each with its proper sphere in which it was autonomous. But the religious divisions in Europe, the absolutist tendencies of rulers generally, the acceptance of the Machiavellian theory that the state is subject to no moral law, the teaching of Bodin on the absolute sovereignty of the state— these led governments to attempt to reduce the Church to a department of state, with half-hearted attempts on the part of Catholics to put the Church on top, and with rare interludes of peace. It nearly always happened in the more modern times that the arena of conflict was the schools.

It was the French Revolution which broached the idea of separation of the church and the state, but the very first law of separation of February 21, 1795, showed that it was not really separation that was sought, but a new kind of union, the complete subjection of the church to the state and of the school to the state. The same idea of "separation" returned again and again: in 1871 under the Commune, and as late as the Law of Separation of 1905. Mexico, Spain, and Portugal followed the same line, usually preached and enforced by political Masonry.

It was only in the United States that a complete political solution had been found, as we have seen, on purely American civil and political grounds in the name of religious freedom, not separation. Tocqueville had come and admired it in the 1830s, and preached it to his contemporaries, but his voice went little heeded.

As in so many other ways late in this third period, Leo XIII pioneered a new path by pointing the way back to the old one. It was he who recalled to the world the original formula of his predecessor, St. Gelasius I. Here is one way in which Pope Leo expressed the idea:

"The Almighty has divided the charge of the human race between two powers, the ecclesiastical and the civil, the one being set over divine, the other over human, things. Each in its kind is supreme, each has fixed limits within which it is contained, limits which are defined by the nature and special object of the province of each, so that there is, we may say, an orbit traced out within which the action of each is brought into play by its own native right." [7]

Here is the official statement on the fundamental relations of church and state. Both are independent in their own special spheres; each one respects the other within the sphere of the other; the sphere of the state is human things, that of the Church divine; each revolves in its orbit "by its own native right." They are, in a word, two distinct societies.

But Leo continues. This distinction between church and state, by the very nature of the two, requires co-operation as well, since "each of these two powers has authority over the same subjects." They must, therefore, co-operate; otherwise, "two powers would be commanding contrary things, and it would be a dereliction of duty to disobey either of the two," for both state and church come from God, though in different ways. How they co-operate will necessarily be left to circumstances, which will decide whether the co-operation be close and immediate or remote and indi-

[7] "The Christian Constitution of States," in The Great *Encyclical Letters of Leo XIII*, ed. John J. Wynne (1903), p. 114.

rect. The important thing that Leo was thinking of is the conscience of the individual. A divided allegiance is always a tragedy, as, for instance, in Italy before the Lateran Treaties; it always means a divided conscience.

Distinction and co-operation. These are the instruments the Catholic Church offers with which to work out in the concrete the eternal dilemma of the claims of the temporal and the eternal, a dilemma that faces every believer. They are better words than separation and union. Neither of these latter two words has any clear meaning, and, not having this, they have led to innumerable misunderstandings. Separation of the two societies— church and state—is, as we have seen, impossible in its literal sense; that is why it has so many divers non-literal ones, at the whim of the speaker. Union also, in its literal sense, is impossible to fulfill except by making the church a department of state, as in Czarist Russia, or by making the two only separate aspects of a single entity, as in the early Middle Ages.

The church and the state are distinct societies. They should also co-operate, for the good of the citizen who is also a member of the church. Separation and union are antitheses to each other;

they cannot exist together. They contradict each other. Distinction and co-operation are correlatives; they must exist together. They necessarily mean peace.

Chapter Seven

The United States and Religion

STARTING from the ideas expressed by the two words, distinction and co-operation, we are now prepared to examine their meaning and application in the tradition of the United States.

The philosophy of the state espoused by the Founding Fathers may be expressed thus: They saw the state as the supreme society in the temporal order which has as its immediate function to promote and protect the well-being on this earth of the members who compose it. It should be furnished with the appropriate political organs to this end: legislative, executive, judicial. The operation of these organs is circumscribed within the limits of the end which the state has before it: the temporal well-being of its members. Hence, it should have a written constitution, and so these limits would have a further circumscription. This would be true either of the individual States or of the United States. The state, therefore, may not go outside the bounds of these limits, which are derived partly from its nature as *a* state and partly from its character as *this* state.

In accord with this theory, in the United States (whatever might have been said of the individual States), supernatural religion—the relation of man with God in the present order—lies outside the competence of our government, as thus conceived. It may not pronounce on dogma; it may not prescribe rites; neither may it forbid worship or interfere with its free practice. Doctrines, rites, worship—these lie outside the orbit of the state. On the other hand, the state, being founded on reason and the natural law, is not, either in its members or its head, exempt in its operations from the precepts of morality dictated by the natural law itself, which is the law of God. Virtue was one of the words most often on the lips of our public men.

This view of the state as a natural society has also been the general teaching of the recent Popes, following St. Thomas Aquinas, about the nature of the state. In 1873, Pius IX said in his Encyclical, *Etsi multa luctuosa:*

"Faith teaches us, and human reason demonstrates, that there is a dual order of things and that therefore we must distinguish two kinds of powers on earth: one of natural origin which looks after the tranquillity of human society and secular affairs, the other of supernatural origin which presides over the City of God, the Church of Christ, and which was divinely instituted for the peace of souls and their eternal salvation." [1]

Thus, from reason we learn of a natural society whose end is civil peace and temporal happiness; from faith, of a supernatural society whose end is interior peace and eternal happiness. Leo XIII also made this doctrine the foundation of his teaching.[2]

Pius XI, in his various Encyclicals, frequently returned to this idea. We shall give two instances, both in connection with education. In *Non Abbiamo Bisogno,* writing against Italian Fascism and its totalitarianism in the schools, he nevertheless concedes that the state has rights and duties in education. He observes:

"Such rights and duties are unchallengeable as long as they remain within the limits of the state's

[1] Denzinger-Bannwart-Umberg, *Enchiridion Symbolorum* (1937), n. 1841.

[2] See, for instance, *Great Encyclicals,* p. 115: "One of the two has for its proximate and chief object the well-being of this mortal life; the other the everlasting joys of heaven."

proper competence, a competence which in its turn is clearly indicated and determined by the role of the state, a role which, though certainly not only bodily and material, is by its very nature limited to the natural, the terrestrial, and the temporal." [3]

Again, in his Encyclical, *On Education*, speaking of the rights of the state in the schools, he said:

"These rights have been conferred upon civil society by the Author of nature Himself, not by the title of fatherhood, as in the case of the Church and the family, but in virtue of the authority it possesses to promote the common temporal welfare, which is precisely the purpose of its existence." [4]

Pius XII, while still Cardinal Pacelli, wrote that "the competence of the state is limited to the natural order," [5] and in his first Encyclical carried on this tradition when he said that the common good which is the end of the state

"can neither be defined according to arbitrary ideas nor can it accept for its standard primarily the material prosperity of society, but rather it

[3] See *Social Wellsprings*, ed. Joseph Husslein (1942), p. 245.
[4] *Ibid.*, p. 100.
[5] Letter to M. Duthoit, in *L'Action Catholique* (July 12, 1933), p. 505.

should be defined according to the harmonious development and the natural perfection of man. It is for this perfection that society is designed by the Creator as a means." [6]

With regard to religion, the Constitutional Convention and the First Congress might have been faced with one of three general situations.

If all the citizens of the United States professed the same religion individually, they would probably have felt there was nothing to prevent them from professing the same religion collectively, *provided* the political organs of the state did not presume to interfere with the doctrines, rites, and worship of that religion, and the ecclesiastical authorities did not meddle in purely political matters. Most of the colonies, in fact, had built their political institutions on this assumption, and some of the new States continued to do so for some time. It has always been held among us that the forms a state takes (outside of a tyranny or despotism imposed from above) depend on the consent of the governed.

A second situation between church and state might have existed here, where the vast majority professed the same religion and a minority pro-

[6] Encyclical *Summi Pontificatus* (1939), N. C. W. C. edition, n. 54.

fessed a different one. Such a situation already existed in several of the States, and the vast majority of Americans felt that, both in the States and in the United States as a whole, the state would have certain definite obligations to the minority.

First of all, it could not take coercive means to make members of the minority embrace the religion or attend the church of the majority. This was implied in their whole concept of the state as they accepted it.

This, incidentally, is also a first precept of the Catholic Church, based on one of its fundamental dogmas. This dogma is that the basic religious act the Christian adult makes, the act of faith, is necessarily a free act, both externally and internally. No external forces may extort it from him. If he should make it under duress, it would be null and void, and the one who extorted it would be guilty of a grave sin of injustice. As Leo XIII said, "the Church is wont to take earnest heed that no one shall be forced to embrace the Catholic faith against his will, for, as St. Augustine wisely reminds us, 'Man cannot believe otherwise than of his own free will.' " [7]

Another obligation which Americans to this

[7] "Christian Constitution of States," in *Great Encyclicals*, p. 127.

day have admitted as binding on the state is that it may not force a minority to make a collective profession of a religion in which it does not believe, any more than it can force its members to profess it individually.

It also happens that this position is in accord with a teaching on the nature of the state as taught in Catholic schools. The state is by its nature a society of individuals willing the same end collectively, and carrying it out by joint action, under the direction of an authority whose power is the power of the community itself. Its unity consists in a public profession of many wills dynamically willing the same common end. Nowadays, this common will is expressed in a Constitution, which has its force from the consent of *all* the members of the state. That the consent of all citizens is required is clear from the fact that the state may require on occasion any of its members to take an oath to the Constitution.

The Founding Fathers felt that, if that Constitution were to have inserted in it a profession of belief in any one religion, this would entail a profession of that religion by all the members, and that would be an obvious violation of the rights of conscience of that minority which did not happen to believe in that religion. It would make them, as part of the community, profess that religion. Membership in an organized community implies an essential part in willing the fundamental act of the community: its fundamental law.

The actual situation which confronted this nation in 1789 was, however, that a number of religious professions existed, no one of them a majority. It seemed to the early Americans an obvious conclusion that the state as a whole might not collectively profess any one of them. It was considered an immoral act for any minority to exact from a majority, as a part of their adhesion to the aims of the state, a collective act of profession in a religion in which they as individuals did not believe. The very act of citizenship would be hypocrisy, for a section of that citizenship would have to profess, externally and as a part of the organized community, a set of beliefs to which they could not conscientiously subscribe. The state, as they saw it and as they were actually setting it up, would not have this power within its competence.

In this historical situation (and it is the case of most states today) they concluded that it was the clear obligation of a state not to exact a public and collective profession of the faith of any one of a number of competing religious denominations. This was the necessary conclusion adopted by the Founding Fathers of the United States. It was not at all an act of political opportunism, but the only possible course of action they could have taken in accord with fundamental justice and with the concept of the state which they were actually creating.

It was with this third situation in mind that the present Pope, Pius XII, on October 6, 1946, in the course of a series of annual addresses he is making on political science to the Supreme Tribunal of the Roman Rota, said:

"The increasingly frequent contacts between different religious professions, mingled indiscriminately within the same nation, have caused civil tribunals to follow the principles of tolerance and liberty of conscience. In fact, there is a political tolerance, a civil tolerance, a social tolerance, in regard to adherents of other religious beliefs which, in circumstances such as these, is a moral duty also for Catholics." [8]

In this connection, it is interesting to note the following considered statement of the American Council on Education:

"The core of meaning in the doctrine of separation of church and state we believe to be this:

[8] See translation in *Clergy Review* (London), April, 1946.

there shall be no ecclesiastical control of political functions; there shall be no political dictation in the ecclesiastical sphere, except as public safety or public morals may require it." [9]

Catholics can accept this statement, and can trace its legitimacy from Pius XII and Leo XIII back to Pope St. Gelasius at the end of the fifth century. To revert to a quotation made earlier from a non-Catholic source, Dr. F. Ernest Johnson said: "To ignore the distinction in function between church and state would be disastrous both to religious and political freedom." This statement could be documented copiously from religious and secular history. Let us note with agreement the phrase, "the distinction in function between church and state," and proceed. It is distinction rather than separation that has any real meaning in the American political tradition.

Consequently, when the United States treats all religions as equal before it, it does not pronounce that all religions are equally true, or equally valid —or equally false, for that matter. It says nothing at all. It does not enter into theology. It considers it has no right to enter there. It grants equality in the interests of its own peculiar secular end,

[9] *The Relation of Religion to Public Education* (November, 1946), p. 25.

which, as St. Thomas said, is the *unitas pacis,* the unity of peace, which ultimately is the common temporal good. This it has the duty of securing before all else, as a state. It does not, or at least should not, grant equality in the name of religious indifferentism ("all ways to God are equally good"). If it did profess indifferentism as a doctrine, it would cease to be wholly a state; it would become partly a church. And this, by its Constitution, it has no competence to do. It has been granted no right to have its members profess collectively, as a condition of being full-fledged citizens, a religious doctrine which it has no right to force them to profess individually.

Jacques Maritain, French Ambassador to the Vatican, has made some penetrating remarks on this. Professing the same theory of the modern state which has been outlined here, he writes:

"There is only one temporal common good, that of political society, as there is only one supernatural common good, that of the Kingdom of God, which is supra-political. To inject into political society a special or partial common good, the temporal common good of the faithful of one religion, even though it were the true religion, and which would claim for them a privileged position in the state, would be to inject into political society a divisive principle and, to that extent, to jeopardize the temporal common good."

What is important to note in this quotation is the pregnant phrase, "a special or partial common good." When a state confers privileges on the faithful of one religion, it is, of course, a temporal good; there is no other kind it can confer; but it is only a partial good in reference to the whole body politic, for whose *total* interest it exists. If all the members of the state were of one religion it could be expected to favor that religion, for the temporal good of the faithful of that religion would then coincide with the total common good of all. But when, as in the United States, the citizens are faithful of different religions, then liberty and equality are the requisites. As Maritain adds:

"For the very reason that political society has more perfectly differentiated its proper sphere and its temporal object, and in actual fact gathers together within its temporal common good men belonging to different religious families, it has become necessary that in the temporal domain the principle of equality of rights be applied to these different families." [10]

[10] Jacques Maritain, *The Rights of Man and Natural Law*, (1943), pp. 26, 27.

It is to be noted, however, that this American principle of liberty and equality of religions before our state, based on its temporal nature, does not mean that it may not confer its temporal benefits on the faithful of those religions, provided it confers them equally and with due regard to their liberty. It is here we see the hollowness and falsity of a theory of separation of church and state which would command the state to withhold its temporal benefits from the adherents of religion *merely because they are religions*. When the state does this, it is not fulfilling its destiny of caring for the total common good of its citizens. Separation in that sense works actual harm to the state itself, which is thus made to do only a part of its total duty, the temporal common welfare of all citizens without regard to their particular condition in life.

Perhaps many of our difficulties in the United States in recent times have arisen from a failure to distinguish between separation as a principle and as a policy. It has been well said in a Protestant publication:

"I suggest that the basic *principle* is freedom, and that the separation of church and state is a political *policy* designed to effectuate religious freedom on the one hand and political freedom on the other. As a policy it grows out of practical necessity due to the fact that our population is religiously heterogeneous. If we were all of one faith the distinction between church and state would be only a functional one: 'separation,' in its present context, would be unknown. Thus, espousal of the separation of church and state by a religious group is not the affirmation of a religious principle, but is rather acceptance of a public policy designed to protect religious freedom and to prevent the domination of the state, at any level, by any church or any combination of churches."[11]

So much for the distinction between church and state. The complementary side of the picture, as I have pointed out, is co-operation. Co-operation means mutual help among two toward the end of each other.[12] In its simplest and widest

[11] F. Ernest Johnson, "Some Crucial Contemporary Issues," *Social Action* (November 15, 1947), p. 14.

[12] In the same issue of *Social Action*, Dean Luther A. Weigle of Yale Divinity School says: "The separation of church and state . . . means that church and state are mutually free, and that neither may rightfully control the other. It does not mean that church and state, being mutually free, may not co-operate with each other. And it does not mean that the state acknowledges no God, or that the state is exempt from the moral law wherewith God sets the bounds of justice for nations as well as individuals" (p. 12). Dean

modern form, this is done by the state in establishing the material and political conditions under which religion can best and most freely flourish, as it does in the United States, and by the church informing its members spiritually to the virtues of citizenship, and especially by its teaching that the authority of the state comes from God.

One specific way in which church and state co-operate, or at least should co-operate, is in the field of education. The state imposes compulsory education on all the young among its members, knowing that an alert, informed electorate is the only atmosphere in which liberty can flourish. When a church, for conscientious reasons, sets up within the state its own system of schools, it is making an important contribution to the ends and purposes of the state. It meets all the requirements of the state in the secular field, but even, and perhaps especially, the *religious* aspects of church education contribute conspicuously to citizenship, because these place civic duties on the most cogent of all foundations, religious obligation.

When the public nature of the education given in church schools is ignored, as it sometimes is nowadays, and the state refuses to do its part in return

Weigle makes it clear enough that it is the church's prerogative to interpret this moral law to the state.

for what it receives, the necessary co-operation between the two is broken down. It remains a one-sided contribution by the church alone. The church does its duty to the state; the state ignores the essential mutuality of the obligation. And by so much the state fails also in its duty to the total common good.

To read some of the polemical literature on this subject, one would get the idea that there was some set principle of separation operating in the United States from the beginning, and that our present system worked itself out logically from that principle. Some of the Justices in the Supreme Court seemed to labor from the same impression in the New Jersey bus-fare case. We have shown in the first four chapters that there is no historical foundation for this assumption.

Justice Holmes once said that the life of the law has not been logic, but experience. The same might be said of the development of American religious liberty. If there was a principle at work, it was the simple and all-embracing one of freedom, guided by political prudence. It is almost entirely in the light of experience gained in making liberty work that, up to our own days, our governments, including the courts, have safeguarded the religious liberties of our people. Whatever the controversialists were saying and doing, the organs of our government were thinking of the equality and liberty of the members of the religious denominations, not of a theological disputation.

To the minds of many it has become a theological disputation. According to these, the First Amendment embodies the "principle of the separation of church and state."

"Then the confusion begins. Imperceptibly it is assumed that the First Amendment is a theological document—a sort of dogmatic decree that lays down a rule of faith. Thereafter it suddenly appears that the First Amendment implicitly 'established,' as the obligatory belief of the American people, the doctrine that all churches are simply voluntary societies, of equally human origin and of equal value in the sight of God, each of them offering to man an equally good way to eternal salvation. In other words, it appears that the First Amendment canonizes Liberal Protestant ecclesiology in an extreme form, and anathematizes as un-American all dissenters." [13]

It ought to be obvious that the kind of theocratic thinking involved in the state of mind described so acutely in this quotation has nothing

[13] John Courtney Murray, S. J., "Separation of Church and State," *America,* 76 (December 7, 1946), p. 261.

in common either with any tenable theory of the state or with the actual progress of the American state as we know it. Yet, it is this attempt to read a *theological*, not a political, meaning into an Amendment to the Federal Constitution that has bedeviled this whole question. The whole effort of the Founding Fathers, the legislatures, and the courts up to the dissents in the Jersey bus-fare decision, has been to establish the liberty and equality of all religious believers before the state. To make the First Amendment a servant of a particular Protestant sectarian position is a monstrous distortion of both historical and political fact. The whole point of the First Amendment was that it was not theological, and that it forbade the American government to be a theologian.

It has been well pointed out that the essential ethical basis of the First Amendment is a recognition of the dualism of man himself:

"Every individual is a civic person, a member of organized society, subject to the authority of its government, ordained to its earthly end. And every individual is likewise a religious person, a creature of God, subject to the authority of conscience, and ordained to an end transcending time. This dualism is inherent in the very nature of man. And every man has the right to have his nature respected for what it is. As citizens of a state, therefore, all men, whatever their religion, have the right to be equal in their civil liberties and in the freedom of their access to all the benefits of organized society. As religious men, all citizens have equal right, *as against the state*, to follow in every rational way the will of God as it is known to them through conscience.

"The First Amendment recognizes this dual set of rights, as flowing from man's dual capacity. Consequently it forbids government so to legislate as to establish distinctions in citizenship on grounds of religious belief; a man's religion cannot be made a civic asset or liability. Similarly, government is forbidden so to legislate as to coerce religious conformity as the condition of civic equality; a man's civic status cannot be made to depend on his religion. The civic person and the religious person are to be separate in law as they are distinct in nature." [14]

Thus, we establish the First Amendment and "separation" of church and state on a purely ethical basis, solely derived from reason, with no distinctly Catholic or Protestant theological overtones. What has been taking place almost unnoticed in recent years, however, has been the at-

[14] *Ibid.*, p. 262.

tempt to transform this basis from its original one to another derived from nineteenth-century European Liberalism, and to identify the American theory of the state with this new theological theory.

Chapter Eight

Liberalism versus Religion

THIS Liberalism held two principal tenets: the absolute autonomy of the human reason; the juridical omnipotence of the state. By the first it held "that the individual is entirely free to profess whatever religion he pleases, or none at all; . . . it is equally permissible for the individual, at his own pleasure, to worship God or not worship Him," [1] meaning, of course, that he is free *before God* to do this. From this it deduced that all religious groups joined by these individuals are of purely human origin and voluntary organizations, for religion is a purely private matter. As for the second tenet, it followed that the state, having its ultimate basis on human reason, and on no law of God, is entirely free from the moral law, or any

[1] Encyclical *Libertas Humana,* in *Great Encyclicals,* pp. 149, 155.

religious consideration whatsoever, and may impose its arbitrary will on all. It is, in other words, atheist by its nature. Therefore, when it does grant freedom to the churches, it grants it out of complete indifference to any of them. It is, of course, the doctrine of Macchiavelli in a modern guise. Separation of church and state in this sense is not a political premise, but a theological one, based on a theory of the nature of the *church*, not of the state.

Fundamentally, therefore, this Liberal theory obviously confuses two different things. It holds as a doctrinal religious dogma that man owes his sole allegiance to his own reason, none to God, unless he chooses to give it to Him. This is freedom of conscience in the Liberal tradition. It is freedom *from* religion, not freedom *of* religion; it is freedom of conscience as against God. Freedom *of* religion is freedom of the individual conscience against the state, a very different thing. *The very reason why man has freedom of religion against the state is precisely because he has no freedom as against God.* He has religious rights as against the state precisely because he has a duty to God, which the state may not destroy, and which, therefore, he has a right to assert against the state.

This concept of religious freedom is the ancient

Christian one. As Pope Leo XIII said, freedom of conscience

"can also be understood in this sense, that *within the political community* a man is free to follow the will of God and do what it commands, out of a moral sense of his duty, without having obstacles put in his way. This is a true freedom, worthy of the sons of God. It is a most reasonable safeguard of the dignity of the human person, and it is superior to all force and injury. This freedom has always been desired by the Church, and is particularly dear to her." [2]

This is the same sense in which the whole Christian world, including the Founding Fathers, has always understood freedom of conscience—freedom before the state, not freedom before God, which no man has. To introduce this latter theological aberration as an American constitutional principle is to distort the whole history of the United States. It is perhaps because some Protestants have not adverted to the real historical meaning of this movement that they have joined with secularists and state absolutists in trying to make the Federal Constitution preach a theological doctrine that would undermine their whole religious position. F. Ernest Johnson has pointed out the

[2] *Ibid.*, pp. 155-156. (Italics mine.)

"ironical situation" that churchmen and secularists are allies in this matter. "I cannot avoid the feeling," he remarks, "that there is something wrong in this picture." Perhaps what has been said here has shown what is wrong.

The complete *reductio ad absurdum* of the new theory of separation of church and state, which has replaced religious liberty and equality in the state in the minds of many people, is the non-sectarian bus.

" 'Where do you go to school?' asked the driver. Raising her little head proudly the child said, 'I'm a new pupil at St. Peter's.' The driver rose from his seat and put his arm across the aisle. 'Wait a minute. You can't ride in this bus, little lady. We only carry public-school kids. *This is a non-sectarian bus!*' The other children laughed. One boy said, 'Aw, let her ride today.' 'It's against the law,' said the driver. 'Off you go, little girl. Sorry.' " (Marjorie walked three miles to school in the rain her first day.)

If this sounds like *Alice in Wonderland*, do not blame the writer of the story.[3] It could have happened in most places, and probably, except for the

[3] William E. McManus, "The Non-sectarian Bus," *Columbia*, April 1947; also separately published as a pamphlet by the N. C. W. C.

actual dialogue, has often happened.[4] In the course of the magazine story, Marjorie's father, Mr. James Ryan (a groceries salesman) later delivered himself at a county school-board meeting of an interesting and pertinent speech. In this speech, he aligned himself with "all loyal Americans" who do not believe that church and state should be controlled by each other. The things that are God's and the things that are Caesar's are still in separate spheres. But how can this doctrine be used as an excuse for putting a Catholic child off a public school bus? It is straining the First Amendment beyond all reason when it makes church membership a liability for an American citizen.

In the Everson case, Justice Rutledge admitted in his dissent that an interpretation of the First Amendment forbidding all state subsidies for matters connected in some way with religion does indeed work a hardship upon those citizens who do not, for instance, use the public schools. But, one may ask in all fairness: What is the difference between discrimination (which the First Amend-

---

[4] Since the above was written it did happen, except that the bus driver resigned rather than pass Catholic-school children in King County, Washington, when the State Superintendent of Public Instruction ordered all Catholic children out of school buses supported by taxes (NCWC News Service, January 31, 1948).

ment certainly forbids) and a "hardship"? Why should the First Amendment work a hardship anyway? And, if the hardship ensues because the citizen is following the precepts of his church, is not that interfering with the free exercise of his religion?

Mr. Ryan had probably not read the majority decision of the Mississippi Supreme Court in a free textbook case, but he echoed its words:

"Useful citizenship is a product and servant of both the church and the state, and the citizen's freedom must include the rights and benefits of each, and to import into each the ideals and training of the other. [Note the point of distinction and co-operation.] *There is no requirement that the church should be a liability to those of its citizenship who are at the same time citizens of the state.* . . . Indeed, the state has made historical acknowledgment and daily legislative admission of a mutual dependence, one upon the other. It is the *control* of one over the other that the Constitution forbids." [5]

It would seem that here we have the ultimate showdown on this fallacious issue of separation of church and state. Separation has been pushed to

[5] *Chance* v. *Mississippi*, 190 Miss. 453; 200 So. 706. (Italics mine.)

such a length that religion has become a civic liability. A speaker at a Congressional hearing on Federal aid for schools actually opposed the Federal lunch program for Catholic-school children, on the ground that it violated the "principle of separation of church and state." Another would forbid public-health services—vaccination, tuberculosis X-rays and the like—to children who go to parochial schools, for the same reason. It has been asked in deadly seriousness and with entire reason whether *any* public service (a traffic policeman at a Catholic school crossing) can be permitted, on the same ground.

This question can be enlarged with all logic and justice. The public sidewalks leading to a non-public school, the public playground located on public-school property, vaccination by a public-school doctor, the public sewer draining off waste from a parochial school, the public library as an adjunct to parochial-school work, the public hospital's services for injuries received on parochial-school premises—are all these, because they are publicly tax-supported, to be refused to parochial-school children?

Again, the *reductio ad absurdum*. But, the absurdity lies not in the *reductio;* it lies in the so-called "principle" which it debunks. What is absurd in its conclusions is absurd in its premises, and the premise is that the Federal Constitution by its First Amendment intended to introduce a kind of second-class citizenship by reason of religion, whereas what it really intended to do was to establish the equality and liberty under the law of all religions. Catholic parents pay taxes for schools and other public services, but, because they also have a religious obligation to send their children to church schools, these children of theirs are excluded from the benefits accruing from those taxes.

No Catholic parent has yet sued to show that his religious liberty is violated by using his taxes exclusively for only one kind of school, a school to which his church and his religious conscience forbids him to send his children. But why not? If Catholics had been like other groups, the Supreme Court would long since have been clogged with cases demanding that the religious liberty of Catholic citizens be respected by school boards, which refuse to grant public services to parochial-school children. The answer is that here we are dealing with schools, and the public school is sacred to "the principle of separation of church and state."

Let us examine this. The issue must be faced.

First of all, we have to rule out the idea that the "public" school has a monopoly of public education. Only the totalitarian state has ever claimed this right. Besides, the United States Supreme Court has once and for all ruled, in the Nebraska and Oregon cases, that the parent fulfills his admitted obligation to the state when he sends his child to a school of his own choice.

The second piece of deadwood that has to be cleared away is the charge that, somehow, the parochial school does not qualify as public education, that it is, in fact, merely another Sunday school prolonged throughout the week. State and county educational authorities, accrediting boards and the like know better, but it is a point constantly obscured in controversy, at Congressional hearings, and in some Protestant church-board resolutions. The secular education given in the parochial school is the same as the education given in public schools, as required by State compulsory-education laws and governed by State educational standards. The Catholic child, in attending the parochial school, is complying with the State's laws. No State authority has ever questioned this. The fact that, *over and above this,* the secular education is enriched and illumined by religious teaching and spiritual motivation is something of which our government may not take account, such things being outside its ken by its Constitution. As far as its special action is concerned, these things do not exist.

This position, that the parochial school performs a public function, can be overturned only on two assumptions: that the state may forbid the intermingling of religion with the secular education which it requires; or, what comes to almost the same thing, that the parochial school is itself a violation of a principle of church and state, stretched to its widest, which means a compulsory and complete divorce of religion from any institution performing a public service—both of which assumptions are absurd on the face of them. Certainly, no believer of whatever faith could admit them.

The third obstacle on the road to understanding is the assumption that no money collected by the state in taxes may go to any activity connected with religion. Apart from the fact that this assumption has no basis in American tradition, it is also inconsistent with present American practice and American law. Public funds have been distributed to church institutions through the NYA Act, the so-called G.I. Bill of Rights, the Mead Housing Act, the Lanham Act, the School Lunch

Act; public funds go to chaplains in Army and Navy, to chaplains in public hospitals, to chaplains in Senate and House of Representatives, to such diverse institutions as the Carville Leprosarium and Howard University; state-paid policemen guard children at street crossings, parochial schools have ordinary fire and police protection, medical aid, sewage and trash disposal, use of highways and sidewalks; religious and educational institutions enjoy a state subsidy in the form of tax exemption; some parochial-school children ride free or at reduced rates on municipally owned traction lines; free text books and bus transportation are given them in some schools.

This list of instances of co-operation between the state furnishing funds and a religious institution furnishing public service could be prolonged indefinitely in thousands of local areas. But enough have been given to show beyond a doubt that there does not exist (or ever has existed) a principle which forbids Federal funds to go to religious institutions, if they are performing a public service.

In so many and diverse fields of co-operation between church and state it seems strange that only when it comes to be a question of sharing money with the schools is there violent opposition, and the appeal to a non-existent principle. Those who invoke separation of church and state in this matter, while tolerating its violation in so many other ways, are entirely inconsistent in still another way also: they oppose Federal funds to other non-public but non-sectarian schools, showing that separation of church and state is not the real issue. Is the real issue a desire to maintain a monopoly of the public school's control of public money, and, so far as the objectors are churchmen, a hope to retain control of the public school?

This whole debate resolves itself into this dilemma: Either the parochial schools perform the same function as the public schools in training children for American citizenship, or they do not. If they do, they are worthy of public support in return for the contribution they make to the state; if they do not perform the same function, then they should immediately be deprived of approval under State compulsory-education laws. There is no danger of this second contingency happening; it would immediately be recognized as a monstrous perversion of justice by Catholic and non-Catholic alike, and not least by the State school authorities themselves. The very suggestion of such an action would bring into clear light the fact that the parochial schools do perform the public function which the laws require.

That Catholics are making a tremendous, but too-little-known contribution to the welfare of the country in education is clear from the figures. In 1944, there were 2,507,501 children in 10,225 Catholic elementary and secondary schools, staffed by 84,342 teachers. This great school system is supported almost entirely by voluntary contributions.

These figures are not rhetoric. They pose to the people of the United States a serious problem. We have here two situations. A church which has as members more than 25,000,000 people in the United States teaches that they can fulfill their obligations to the state in education by maintaining parochial schools. Yet, in this tremendous contribution to public welfare, they receive little or no direct remuneration from the beneficiary, the people of the United States. The answer to this manifest injustice is distinction, but also co-operation, between the church and the state, which bring unity and the common good, not a trumped-up fallacy of separation *vs.* union, which only divides our citizenry.

The legal position that lies behind the logic of this chapter was well set forth by Justice Alexander of the Mississippi Supreme Court in a textbook case:

"The religion to which children of school age adhere is not subject to control by the state; but the children themselves are subject to its control. If the pupil may fulfill its duty to the state by attending a parochial school, it is difficult to see why the state may not fulfill its duty by encouraging it 'by all suitable means.' The state is under the duty to ignore the child's creed, but not its need. It cannot control what one child may think, but it can and must do all it can to teach the child how to think. The state which allows the pupil to subscribe to any religious creed should not, because of his exercise of this right, proscribe him from benefits common to all." [6]

[6] *Ibid.*

Chapter Nine

False Definitions of Separation

IN THE preceding chapters of this study we have considered two things: (1) the original Constitutional meaning of separation of church and state and of religious liberty in the United States; and (2) the true sense in which separation finds support in the American tradition.

We now have to take up an examination of several positions which are opposed to that taken here, and to assay their validity, particularly as they have been set forth in recent Supreme Court cases dealing chiefly with education, and in certain Congressional hearings on pending bills.

The opposing positions fall into several categories. The first of these does not properly belong here at all, but, because it has often been mentioned in Congressional hearings and elsewhere, it may be mentioned merely to get it out of the way. This is the position of those who are not so much opposed to public support of church schools as they are opposed to those schools themselves.

For instance, John H. Cowles, Grand Commander of the Scottish Rite Masons, Southern Jurisdiction, in a statement to a House Committee on April 13, 1947, included five points: "What the Supreme Council Favors." The first of these is: "The American public school, non-partisan, non-sectarian, efficient, democratic, *for all of the children of all the people*." This claim of a state monopoly of education has appeared in magazines and statements of the Southern Jurisdiction for very many years. It was, of course, borrowed from political Latin Masonry, in which it has been a slogan and an aim for a century in Italy, France, Spain, Portugal, Mexico, and South America generally, and was copied by the Nazis in Germany and the Soviets in Russia.

This same idea of state monopoly of education was taken up by Max Lerner in an article entitled, "School Aid and the Trojan Horse." In the course of this article he said:

"It is true that dangerous inroads have already been made on the principle of the separation of church and state. The first step was taken when the Supreme Court decided that a religious group could not be compelled to send its children to the public schools, and that it could run its own school at its own expense." [1]

He apparently refers to the Oregon school case, and shows a sublime disregard for the whole of American history, during which the right of freedom of education was unquestioned.

This extreme position is mentioned here only because one finds it innocently echoed by otherwise well-intentioned and religious-minded people, who seem unaware of the implications of what they are saying. One of the forms this takes is the statement that the public school is "the bulwark of democracy," and other similar expressions, with the implied or stated meaning that somehow the Catholic parochial school is undemocratic, or even anti-democratic. The unspoken conclusion is that, therefore, the parochial school should not be tolerated. Thus, Dr. Samuel McCrea Cavert, General Secretary of the Federal Council of Churches, remarked before a House committee hearing: "To provide Federal funds for parochial schools would be to encourage segregated educational systems, and thereby threaten our democracy by fragmentizing our culture." He also quoted Bishop G. Bromley Oxnam, former President of the Federal

[1] See *PM* (New York), May 18, 1947.

Council: "Public support for parochial schools would divide the community into sectarian educational systems and destroy the unity essential as democracy faces the totalitarian threat of freedom."

This idea that a totalitarian democracy (under the specious plea of "unity") is the only thing that can save freedom is not a new one among many unbelieving secularists. What is surprising is to hear a plea for a monolithic society coming from religious men, for that is the very thing that would destroy them and all that they stand for. One can only believe that they have not examined all the terrible implications of the stand they have been taking along this line, not once, but many times, in public and in private.

Dr. Lerner had a clearer view of what is aimed at, for he added in the passage quoted above: "Two values conflicted here: the nation's stake in having a common democratic education for its children, and the principle of freedom of conscience in education. The latter won—whether rightly or wrongly it is now too late to decide." Dr. Lerner, at least, had decided that freedom of conscience had won out wrongly. A "democracy" that must defeat freedom of conscience to save itself is what most of the secularists are demanding. Protestant churchmen, at least, might have been expected to maintain that the very pluralism which has distinguished American civilization has been its salvation. Totalitarianism, whether called by the name of "unity," (as, incidentally, Hitler also called it), or by any other name, is destructive of this pluralism.

Akin to this objection, one sees constantly repeated, particularly by the religious objectors to Federal support of private schools, the idea that this support would create a fatal competition to the public schools. It is difficult to understand this objection, for it hardly stands analysis. It means, if it means anything, either that the drive of some secularists to create a state monopoly of education would be irrevocably halted if parochial schools were helped, or it means that children in large masses would flock from the public schools— whither? Certainly, one might expect that more Catholics might attend Catholic schools, but who, besides those who want a monolithic school and will sacrifice freedom of conscience for it, could object to that, either in justice or in law? How many others would leave the public schools? The number who would attend privately owned schools in greater numbers would be negligible, taken from the upper one-tenth of one percent of the population. Those schools are endowed, and not in need of funds. How many others? It would seem to betray a singular lack of confidence in the public schools, if we are to expect that their pupils are to desert them *en masse* when something else is offered. And who would initiate this something else? Certainly not the Protestants, many if not most of whose ministers have expressed complete confidence in the public schools as they are. That appears to leave only the Communists.

In the case of many, this professed fear for democracy and the public schools not very successfully conceals another preoccupation which is far more sinister. To these, separation of church and state means the separation of the state and religion —not religion in the sense of organized religion, but religion itself. The state, no matter what the religious convictions of its members, must be professedly atheist, acknowledging no subjection to the natural law, which is, of course, the law of God as we receive it in our nature.

This is a very different thing from the distinction between church and state which we set forth earlier in this study. We said that the state is a natural society, as distinct from the church which is a supernatural society, operates in the field of the temporal happiness of man, and has no competence in the field of supernatural religion. The theory of the separation of the church and religion completely excludes the correlative of the distinction between the spheres of the two—namely, their necessary co-operation in the field of human relations, since the same persons are largely members of both societies.

This particular theory of church and state, which throughout this study we have called secularism, has had many phases, both in history and at the present day. When it first appeared in the eighteenth century during the so-called Enlightenment, it had a rather Deist tinge; God was certainly the Great Architect of the Universe, but He had not made known His will to man in any tangible form beyond what man could find out by his own unaided reason. Organized religion was a purely historical human invention. Thomas Jefferson was its principal exponent among the politicians of our Revolutionary era.

In the course of the nineteenth century, however, this theory of the church took other and ever more radical forms. In the century previous, John Locke, following some of the early Reformers, had drawn the conclusion that religion is a purely individual matter, and that churches are merely voluntary organizations, depending in no wise on the will of God. Taking up this theological theory, the followers of Jefferson, with considerable encouragement from some writings of Jefferson himself, attempted, with some success, to incorporate it into our constitutional tradition.

In its new form, however, the theory was still a theory of the church and not of the state. It meant that the state—the United States—looked on all forms of organized religion with indifference, and consequently, *by virtue of this theological principle,* as entitled to equality before the state, along with no religion at all, or the denial of religion, atheism. It was actually to pronounce between two parties to a theological controversy.

In other words, what was attempted was to settle the question of our relations of church and state, and even of the state and religion, on a theological premise, not on a legal or constitutional one, on a theory of the church, not on a theory of the state, and to incorporate this theological, sectarian theory into our constitutional jurisprudence. We contend that this is precisely what has been attempted in some recent Supreme Court cases.

At this point we must pause to note that there is a deep theological cleavage, in the realm of purely theological controversy, between Catholics on the one hand, and evangelical Protestants on the other, about the nature of the church itself. In a sense, the Protestant position is somewhat akin to that of the secularists, but not altogether. The traditional Protestant position, *in theory*, was that the church is a purely invisible society, composed of the saved, or of the Elect, or of believers, but not really a true society existing where it can be seen in the world. In practice, of course, this position has long been abandoned. "Organized religion" (a church) is the standard ecclesiastical definition, even among Protestants.

The secularists, however, adhered to the idea of an invisible church, and developed it into the concept of religion as a purely interior and subjective attitude. One was free or not, even before God, to take or leave religion, as one happened to feel about the matter; as far as joining any visible society called the church was concerned, one was also free to join it or not, not only before the state but even in conscience before God. In other words, it was not only freedom *of* religion (before the state), but freedom *from* religion (before God), that was claimed. Most of the secularists have chosen and proclaimed both of these freedoms, and in fact freely confused one with the other. The church is, therefore, a voluntary society only, *and for this reason* the state is indifferent to any church, from a theological premise. Thomas Jefferson, as a Deist, had worked himself into this attitude.

Believing Protestants cannot really accept this position, however much they may seem to adopt it in the church-and-state controversy. However, the rationalistic liberal Protestantism of the nineteenth century comes very close to accepting it. This so-called modernism is an effective solvent of anything like a collective worship or profession of faith. But again, it must be reiterated, it is a theological position, not a political one.

Between this Protestant theory of the church, whether traditional or rationalistic, and the Catholic position, there is a deep and unbridgeable religious chasm. To the Catholic, the Church is a visible, organized, and hierarchical society, tracing its existence, its spiritual jurisdiction over its members, and its orders back to Christ Himself, who founded it and chose the Apostles to administer it and through it to carry on His divine mission. It is, therefore, a public society, and, like the state, what is technically called a "perfect" society, one that has within itself all the means to attain its particular end.

Protestants do not accept this doctrine about the

church. Indeed, the original "protest" (whence their name) was precisely against this doctrine of a living visible church, as the divinely authorized interpreter of the teachings of Christ.

This theological interlude is introduced here because of its capital importance to the general subject we are discussing. At first glance, it may not seem to have any relevance to the question, for instance, of a Supreme Court decision on a bus fare or released time. But it has a deep relevance. It raises, indeed, the question of the competence of the Supreme Court to base a decision on a theological doctrine about the nature of a church. For this is precisely what has been asked. Moreover, the theological doctrine in question is one which very many Protestants are unable to accept, if they really see the implications of it for their own churches. Thus, we see that there exists a deep theological cleavage between Catholics and Protestants on the one hand, and between different groups of Protestants on the other. If the Court were to adopt one of these conflicting doctrines, and make it the basis of a decision or a dissent, it would be departing from the competence of our state, and, in effect, making that very establishment of religion which is forbidden by the First Amendment.

We have already pointed out that what has imperceptibly been taking place is an attempt to make the First Amendment a theological document canonizing Liberal Protestant ecclesiology in an extreme form. Thus we are being told, in effect, that the First Amendment really established a distinct form of religion as an obligatory faith, and all dissenters to this establishment are being anathematized as—religious heretics? No; as un-American. If one does not believe that all religious bodies are simply voluntary societies, of equally human origin, and of equal value in the sight of God, each of them offering to man an equally good way to eternal salvation, and if one refuses to believe that the *state* must be indifferent to all religions on this basis, and not on its nature as a state—a natural society founded on the natural law—then one is disqualified as a good American.

Chapter Ten

Whither the
Supreme Court?

IN THE preceding chapter we have examined some fallacious positions that have been taken with regard to the American tradition of separation of church and state. We have now finally to weigh some similar positions that have been taken in recent years with regard to the First Amendment itself, on which separation of church and state is said to be based.

As we have seen, this Amendment, in its religious clauses, contains two distinct parts: (1) Congress shall make no law respecting an establishment of religion; that is, it may not adopt legislation favoring one or more forms of religion in preference to all others; and (2) Congress shall make no law prohibiting the free exercise of religion; that is, it must respect freedom of conscience and worship. The first part deals with equality; the second, with liberty.

We have seen the simple and clear explanation of what the Amendment intended as given by James Madison, when he said that "he apprehended the meaning of the words to be that Congress should not establish a religion and enforce the legal observation of it by law, nor compel men to worship God in any manner contrary to their conscience."

We have also seen that, up to the Everson and McCollum cases, no attempt was made to extend the establishment-of-religion clause to the States through the Fourteenth Amendment (as the liberty-of-conscience clause has been). The year 1947, however, saw a determined effort made to have the Supreme Court declare that what the First Amendment forbade the Congress to do in the way of establishing a religion was now forbidden to the States as well through the Fourteenth Amendment.

This proposal, however, involves on the face of it a constitutional and historical absurdity. The whole clear and avowed purpose of the First Amendment was to take away from the *Federal* Government power to decide what the relations between government and religion should be, and

to leave that *to the local and State authorities.*
What the new proposal would do would be to
forbid the States to do what the First Amendment
expressly designed that they could and should do,
and thus in effect nullify that part of the Amendment. Thus, whereas the liberty-of-conscience
clause was logically extended to protect individual liberties, the establishment-of-religion clause
would be repealed by judicial action. This result
certainly was never intended by either of the Con-
gresses which proposed the two Amendments.

It might be said that it is idle to argue about
whether the First Amendment, in this part of it,
is extended to the States by the Fourteenth
Amendment, since most of the States already have
forbidden themselves in their Constitutions to establish a religion. This would be a valid objection if
it were not for the fact that the proposal is cou-
pled with a new interpretation of what the First
Amendment means. This new interpretation holds
that what the no-establishment clause really forbids is any use of tax funds for any activity with
which religion is even indirectly connected, even
when the principle of equality of all religions
is preserved. Thus, the no-establishment clause
would be interpreted through the Fourteenth

Amendment as prohibiting the States from making any such use of tax funds.

We have already shown that this interpretation of the First Amendment lacks any historical justification. The only historical argument thus far adduced has been that Madison, in his fight against the Assessment Bill in Virginia and in his *Remonstrance*, held that the state may make no monetary contributions to religious enterprises. Since it was he who introduced what became the First Amendment (adopted after many changes), his writings are the source of our knowledge of what the First Amendment means. We have already shown that what a future Congressman, in a hot fight in his State Legislature, wrote in a pamphlet setting forth his private opinions on disestablishment in Virginia is not to be taken as proving the meaning of an Amendment to the Federal Constitution adopted six years later. In fact, Madison himself did not take that meaning of the First Amendment, nor did his own State of Virginia when it had the Amendment up for ratification. For a historian, that should be enough to disprove this new interpretation of the First Amendment, even if we take Madison and Virginia as our witnesses as to the meaning of the Amendment, as the proponents of the new line of argument have done.

After all, even if the Fourteenth Amendment passes on the First Amendment to the States in its entirety, it cannot pass on anything except what is there.

Akin to this argument is another, based likewise on the history of Virginia and Madison's *Remonstrance,* that it is the sense of the First Amendment that support of any activity with which religion is also connected is a private matter; hence, that it cannot fall under the head of public business which the state might assist out of public monies. This argument was succinctly summarized, for instance, by Justice Rutledge in his dissent in the Everson case. This case, we remind the reader again, had to do with the right of a New Jersey school board to avail itself of a State law allowing parochial-school children to be carried on public-school buses: ". . . education which includes religious training and teaching and its support have been made matters of private right and function, *by the very terms of the First Amendment.*" And again: "The Amendment has removed this form of promoting the public welfare from legislative and judicial competence to make a public function. It is exclusively a private affair." [1]

[1] Supreme Court of the U.S., No. 52, October term, 1946. Ed. cited, pp. 45, 47. (Italics mine.)

It may be admitted that, if we are to take as the meaning of the First Amendment what was said and done by Madison in Virginia some years before, then this interpretation of the First Amendment is valid. It has been amply shown here that the Amendment itself, in its legislative history, has no such meaning, whatever may have been Madison's and Virginia's previous and private opinions. The Amendment did not forbid, in any terms, support of activities connected with religion. What it forbade was *preferential* support, and by the Federal Government.

To give another instance of this enlarging of the meaning of the First Amendment beyond what the records bear, we may cite Justice Jackson in his own dissent in the Everson case. In the course of his reasoning he says:

"There is no answer to the proposition more fully expounded by Mr. Justice Rutledge that the effect of the religious freedom Amendment to our Constitution was to take every form of propagation of religion out of the realm of things which could directly or indirectly be made public business and thereby be supported in whole or in part at the taxpayers' expense." [2]

The answer to Justice Rutledge's argument

[2] *Ibid.*

was, curiously enough, given by Justice Jackson himself in his preceding paragraph. The Court (Justice Black) had observed that policemen and firemen, publicly paid, protect the safety of parochial school children and the property which they frequent. Justice Jackson remarks on this point:

"A policeman protects a Catholic, of course— but not because he is a Catholic; it is because he is a man and a member of our society. The fireman protects the church school—but not because it is a church school; it is because it is property, part of the assets of our society. Neither the fireman nor the policeman has to ask before he renders aid: 'Is that man or building identified with the Catholic Church?' "

Precisely. That is our point. When the state grants support to a Catholic school in some way it is not because it is Catholic; it is because the students are members of our society. When its support affects in some way the school itself, it is not because it is Catholic, but because it is part of the assets of our society. More, even, and equally as logically, it is because the school and everything that goes on in it affect the welfare of our society. That is the reason why, and the only possible reason why, the state may cast its eyes on the parochial school at all. That is why, on Justice Jackson's own showing, the majority of the Court in the Everson decision validly made the distinction between the public service rendered by the parochial school and the religious opinions of the parents who send their children to it. The former is definitely within the purview of the state; the latter is completely out of that purview, as it is with the policeman who is detailed to direct traffic in front of the school, but who indirectly helps the school by making it possible for the children to go safely to and from its classes.

Into this argument, somewhere along the line, has suddenly crept the idea that under the First Amendment the state may not even "indirectly," in whole or in part, support religion by supporting the public service which the religious institution confers. This, we submit, is something new, and if carried out would cripple a whole long series of public services, from Indian Mission schools and leper hospitals to veterans' part-scholarships and chaplains' services, which we doubt the Supreme Court intended to do, for they have never been seriously challenged on this basis. There seems to be no proof alleged to forbid an indirect support of religion, but against this argument we may adduce this, that the state may, under a regime of distinction of church and state, reach religion only inasmuch as religion reaches the state indirectly, and, in the case of the schools, only inasmuch as religious teaching itself affects the state.

Many religious men among Protestants have with increasing emphasis asserted that the religious motive is an essential element of citizenship and have deplored the rise of secularism in this country. Prominent among these, for instance, has been Dr. Charles Clayton Morrison, who recently retired as editor of the *Christian Century,* and since then has been active in a movement to safeguard the First Amendment against what are claimed to be "encroachments" on it by Catholics. Before retiring, Dr. Morrison wrote:

"America's rigidly non-religious public-school system is an ideal training ground for secularism. Unlike Catholicism, the Protestant churches . . . have given to the public school their consistent and unreserved devotion. The result is that their own children have been delivered back to their churches with a mentality that is not only unintelligent about religion but relatively incapacitated even to ask questions out of which religion arises." [3]

Men such as Dr. Morrison may not, and some of them do not, believe that the parochial school is the ideal solution of the problem which they raise,

[3] *Christian Century,* July 8, 1946.

but there still remains implicit in their position the assumption that the religious motive is necessary for good citizenship among the young. Since the parochial school teaches universally, following St. Paul, that the authority of the state is ultimately the authority of God, it gives its pupils the most cogent argument for good citizenship. The other social virtues of justice and charity, the necessity of confession of evil-doing, and similar spiritual exercises that are a part of religious teaching, are a similar indirect contribution to the well-being of the state. It can well be argued that, even on the side of its purely religious teaching, the parochial school makes a potent indirect contribution to the end of the state, one that well deserves an indirect contribution of the state in return.

It would seem, therefore, that this new argument which would remove even indirect support from religious schools is not valid even if we consider their religious teaching itself: their indirect, but no less cogent, contribution to the well-being of the state. There has never been a time, from George Washington's Farewell Address to fairly recent years, when it was denied that religious teaching had an indirect though powerful effect on the peace and prosperity of this Republic. Only a fatal tidal wave of secularism, engulfing and silencing forever the religious-minded men of this country, would raise the level of irreligion to the courts, which have hitherto been the unbreakable dike against it. It would be sad, indeed, if those sincere men who have God's interests at heart would add to this flood by unconsidered utterances.

There are indications that some feel at this point that, whatever be the indirect benefit which the parochial school confers on the state by its religious teaching, there is nothing else about it which could be called a temporal good on which the state is competent to legislate or the courts to pronounce. We have already pointed out the wide misconception which exists in this regard. Even Justice Rutledge, who at one point implies that the parochial school does perform a public service, at another seems to accept this misconception, for he says:

"An appropriation from the public treasury to pay the cost of transportation to Sunday school, to weekday special classes at the church or parish house, or to the meetings of various young people's religious societies, such as the Y.M.C.A., the Y.W.C.A., the Y.M.H.A., the Epworth League, could not stand the constitutional attack."

So far as we know, nobody has ever demanded

appropriations from the public treasury for enterprises analogous to these, and it is doubtful that
such a demand would stand the constitutional attack. But the Justice continues:

"This would be true, whether or not secular activities were mixed with the religious. If such an
appropriation could not stand, then it is hard to
see how one becomes valid *for the same thing upon
the more extended scale of daily instruction.*
Surely constitutionality does not turn on where
or how often the mixed teaching occurs." [4]

Surely, it does not, nor, so far as we know again,
has anyone ever argued that it does. This is simply
to misconstrue just what goes on in a parochial
school. Yet, it seems that this is precisely where
the difficulty lies. Perhaps a visit to a parochial
school would be necessary, to destroy once and for
all this fundamental misconception.

It is certainly not confined to Justice Rutledge,
for many of those who have testified against Congressional measures for Federal support of parochial schools have betrayed the same lack of understanding of the true nature of the parochial
school. To these, also, the instruction given in
the parochial school is "the same thing upon the
more extended scale of daily instruction" as the

[4] *Loc. cit.,* pp. 41-42.

purely religious activities such as the Epworth League, even though "secular activities are mixed with the religious." To anyone even slightly acquainted with the educational standards of those county or state boards that are responsible for the execution of the compulsory-education laws, this idea of the parochial school is slightly ridiculous. If it were true, then every Catholic parent in the land would long ago have been fined or jailed for violating the laws which require that their children receive an education in every respect equivalent to that offered in the public schools. It is for obeying this civil law, and for nothing else, that, even under the First Amendment, the United States is not forbidden to offer support to parents who thus fulfill their duty to the state. This aspect of the matter is the only one which the state is competent to regard, even though those parents are at the same time also fulfilling another obligation which they have to their religion. This second aspect of the matter, however, is outside the competence of the state to consider.

There remain two further misunderstandings of the meaning of the First Amendment which we must consider. They have to do with the interpretation of the words, "establishment of religion."

By the first of these, "establishment" would be

synonymous with "promotion" or "assistance," so that what is forbidden by the phrase is any kind of legislation that might even indirectly assist reli-gion. Here again, the historical evidence is on the other side. If this interpretation were valid, then we would be reading into the Amendment that very hostility to religion which, as we have shown, the First Congress was so anxious to avoid.

The other misunderstanding would make "es-tablishment of religion" the same as a "religious establishment," as we talk of a "dry-goods estab-lishment" or an "undertaking establishment." On this interpretation, again, the Government would be forbidden to make any law concerning religion understood in the sense of a religious institution. Thus, a church, a school, or even an incorporated body would be excluded from any benefits which the state might have to confer. This interpretation has already been rejected by the Supreme Court.[5] Besides, as we have shown, the words, "establish-ment of religion," had, at the time of the adoption of the First Amendment, a well-defined technical meaning—that of a religion preferred by the state before all others.

In all the historical arguments over the meaning

[5] By Justice Peckham, in *Bradfield* v. *Roberts*, 175 U.S. 291 (1899).

of the First Amendment, not the least of the omissions has been the capital fact, which we have already pointed out, that the men who actually made the Constitution were the Federalists. And most of the Federalists, especially George Washington, Alexander Hamilton, John Adams, James Wilson, Gouverneur Morris, and John Marshall, rarely neglected in their public utterances to couple religion and morality with the state, and especially with the schools. The Northwest Ordinance and Washington's Farewell Address are noteworthy instances of this conviction of the necessity of the co-operation of religion and statecraft. Moreover, in the very House in which the First Amendment was adopted there were 52 Federalists to 12 Anti-Federalists, and in the Senate there were 20 Federalists to no Anti-Federalists. Is it likely that they would have passed an Amendment if they thought it had the purely secularist meaning which is now being read into it?

What happened, of course, was that the Jeffersonians won out in the election of 1800, and one school of scholars ever since has been reading back into the Constitution the secularist ideology of Jefferson himself, as if that were its original meaning. That also partly accounts for the constant efforts of this school to blacken the Federalists, and to exaggerate the merits of Jefferson. As a matter of fact, Jefferson had almost nothing to do with the Constitution and the First Amendment, since he was serving his country abroad at the time. To find the meaning of an Amendment we have to study its legislative history. Secondary or later glosses do not give us the whole picture, or even necessarily the accurate picture.

So much for the historical aspect of the First Amendment and the distortions which that aspect has undergone during our time; now, for what we might call its theological aspect. Increasingly, there has come about a tendency to introduce into the Constitution and its interpretation one particular sectarian ecclesiology, and that in an extreme form of secularism in the state, and to make it the established faith of the country. This has been noted also and deplored in some Protestant circles.

What that sectarian theology is we have seen. It is the doctrine of a particular school of liberal Protestants about the nature of religion. Religion, says this school, "is exclusively a private affair." James Madison is quoted in this sense to prove that this is what he held, and held to be the official American Constitutional doctrine.

One might ask: Where does the right arise to ask for a theological pronouncement about the nature of religion in a decision of a United States Court? And by what right may it be claimed to be the official dogma of this nation? There are some Americans who hold this doctrine, of course; there are very many others who do not, even among Protestants. If the First Amendment means anything, it means that the Federal Government may make no such pronouncements. Yet, here, we have the First Amendment invoked to prove the very thing that would destroy it.

We might justly say to the advocates of such a course, as to the Court itself: "We say the Church is a public institution on a par with the state, but operating in an entirely different province. You say it is merely a non-institutional individual attitude, exclusively private. Very well. We have no right under the First Amendment to ask a Federal judge to pronounce that the church is a public institution; neither have you the right to ask him to espouse one Protestant sectarian doctrine about the nature of religion, and make that the basis of a Court decision. He has no constitutional right to make doctrinal religious pronouncements about either side of this religious controversy, and to draw political consequences from it. All he has the right to do is to pass on the secular aspects of any church enterprise, and to legislate or pass judgment on that."

This fallacy of long standing—of defining a civil liberty before the state in terms of the nature of the church, and not in terms of the admitted nature of the kind of state we happen to have— is the key to the many misunderstandings that have confused this issue. The United States is a society whose competence lies in the secular order and not beyond it. It is highly probable that Supreme Court Justices, with their particular religious backgrounds, might be entirely unaware of a religious controversy into which they were unwittingly led, if, in the name of the Federal Government, they were asked to pass judgment on one side of this religious controversy to the detriment of the others.

Thus we see that, from this new theological approach, the First Amendment is just as unassailable as from the historical, if we take it in the sense in which its creators, the members of the First Congress, took it. Its whole purpose was to preserve religion, not to destroy it; to guarantee its freedom to influence society, not to render it impotent. The objective of those who framed it was not to establish secularism as the national official dogma; still less, to enshrine it in our Constitution.

When the Framers voted to guarantee freedom of religion as against the state, they meant that religion would be free to propagate itself. They did not mean that government would put obstacles in the way of its propagation; quite the contrary. When they voted to create equality of all religions before the state, they did not mean to penalize any particular religion; quite the contrary. They were setting up the kind of a national state which would not be competent to pass on religion, or to adopt any specific side of any religious controversy as the official one. They left the relations of government with religious institutions as the affair of the local and State authorities. That is why they forbade the Federal Government to "establish" any religion.

This last point, of course, is the special significance of the latest Supreme Court case to be argued on this issue. This is the McCollum case of December, 1947. It dealt with the released-time program set up by the Champaign, Illinois, Council of Religious Education to enable those parents who wished it to have religious education for their children on the public-school premises in the denomination of their choice—or, in pure rationalism, if they chose. It was challenged by the parent of one child, James Terry McCollum, who carried it to the Supreme Court on the ground that it violated the First Amendment.

The issue was fairly simple. Either the Champaign Plan violated the establishment-of-religion clause, on the ground that that clause forbade any connection at all of government with religion—which we have shown to be an unfounded assumption, or it violated the freedom-of-religion clause. As to the latter, it was shown conclusively in all the preliminary hearings that James Terry's freedom of religion was not violated, first, because he has no religion, and secondly, because the local school board offered to grant facilities even to classes in atheism if they were desired.[6]

Apart from this, however, there was in this case another and perhaps more serious issue involved, and that is the right of the local and State authorities under the First Amendment, and of the highest court in a State to approve a specific arrangement made between a local school board and the various religious denominations on a basis of absolute equality. This right was challenged by those who took the appeal to the Supreme Court

[6] In the decision on the McCollum case, the Court apparently did base its position on the no-establishment clause, and accepted it as applicable to the States in its new interpretation. See Chapter 11.

of the United States, after the Supreme Court of Illinois had unanimously denied the appeal carried to it. What was asked of the Supreme Court of the United States was, in effect, that: (1) for the first time in history, it reach into a local community and annul an arrangement made by the local authorities and approved by the highest State judicial authority; and (2) do this on an entirely new and unhistorical interpretation of the First Amendment.

This local arrangement was created by the democratic process common to our country, and the Supreme Court was asked to substitute its own judicial action for this process. The attempt was an alarming one, especially as it concerns education. Over 7,000 school districts have these or similar arrangements for released time for religious education, and all these are made in accord with our traditional method of local control of educational and religious relations—quite in line with what the First Amendment has always been considered to be. If they were to be overturned by a Supreme Court decision, it could easily be foreseen that the control of education itself would be transferred from local boards to Washington, and to a judicial tribunal. This is what a fallacious notion of separation of church and state and its unwarranted connection with the First Amendment would have achieved.

Furthermore, we should like to discuss this question with those believing Protestants who are aware of the really serious problem that is presented in these pages. It has become more and more clear that religion must be an essential part of the training that is given our young. Not only Protestant clerics, but also very many laymen in consultation with the public authorities of city and State, have expressed their conviction in this regard. One might even say that the movement in this direction is one of the most significant of our time. Religious values are clearly an essential part of total human values, and the total human values are the objective of religious values. The religious motive is more and more accepted as the fundamental motive for citizenship itself.

Fair-minded Protestants, however, must admit that in the course of the years many of their co-religionists have in large part undergone a great deterioration of conviction as to the part religious motivation should play in forming citizenship. Yet, many of them are formulating wishful plans which go back to their early American traditions. In the very early years, those of the making of the Constitution itself, co-operation of the distinct entities of state and church in the United States was taken for granted. Only a very few secularists held the contrary. As for the school, there was no question. "Religion, morality and learning" were the specific objectives of the school for our forefathers, as the Northwest Ordinance and the Farewell Address testify. Even when the public school as we know it now was agitated in the 1840s, there was no question of a separation of the school and religion. The "non-sectarian" religion of Horace Mann and his associates was still religion—the Christian religion in their notion, but not the religion of any particular sect.

It was secularism of public life imported from radical sources in Europe that finally affected our public schools. Yet, Protestants long believed that the reading of the Bible in the public schools would still retain the religious values they cherished, and this has existed even up to our time in many parts of the country, for Bible reading, in the Protestant tradition, has somewhat the same religious significance that the Sacraments have among Catholics. Even that form of religion has in these last days disappeared in most public schools.

What has happened? It has been the thesis of this book that the shibboleth of separation of church and state has been largely responsible, little by little, why many Americans have yielded to the pressure of those who hold that American democracy actually means separation of religion from the state and the education of the child; that this has been the ultimate objective of the doctrine of separation of church and state as preached by the secularists of nineteenth-century Europe. The last disastrous result of this unfortunate evolution would be that our own legislatures and judiciaries would be seduced into enacting into our fundamental law a sectarian and radical theological dogmatism which would end once and for all our whole American tradition of religious liberty and equality.

Chapter Eleven

Whither the
First Amendment?

ON MARCH 8, 1948, the Supreme Court delivered its opinion in the McCollum case. This case, to quote Justice Black, who read the decision of the Court, related "to the power of a State to utilize its tax-supported public-school system in aid of religious instruction, insofar as that power may be restricted by the First and Fourteenth Amendments."

The Board of Education of Champaign, Illinois, had set up a plan by which the parents could, on their own request and at the expense of the local Council on Religious Education, obtain, on public-school premises, instruction in the Protestant, Catholic, or Jewish religion for their children. The plan was challenged by one Vashti McCollum, an avowed atheist, on the ground that it violated the American "principle" of separation of church and state. The case was carried up to the Illinois Supreme Court, which delivered a unanimous opinion that the practice was not a violation of either the State or the Federal Constitution. It was later, after the New Jersey bus decision, and no doubt because of that decision, carried as an appeal from the State Court to the Supreme Court of the United States.

The United States Supreme Court, by a vote of 8 to 1, reversed the State Supreme Court, and remanded the case to it "for proceedings not inconsistent with this opinion." Justice Frankfurter delivered another opinion, and Justice Jackson offered a concurring opinion, while Justice Reed dissented. It will be instructive to examine the various opinions in this case, because they vividly illustrate the facts and doctrines set forth hitherto in this book.

Mr. Black's decision was based on two findings of fact: the Champaign Plan shows (1) "the use of tax-supported property for religious instruction" and (2) "the close co-operation between the school authorities and the religious council in promoting religious education." For these two reasons, he found, the Champaign Plan "falls squarely under the ban of the First Amendment (made applicable to the States by the Fourteenth) *as we interpreted* it in *Everson* v. *Board of Education*." (Emphasis added.)

Now, this interpretation in the Everson case had, as we have shown, for all but its very general statements, no historical or constitutional justification, and Mr. Black alleged none, except the Reynolds case, which on examination proves to support only the general ideas that the Congress may pass no law respecting an establishment of religion or prohibiting the free exercise thereof (the words of the Amendment itself). Nevertheless, Mr. Black, basing his newest decision on his previous decision which itself had no previous basis in a decision, decided that the Champaign Plan was unconstitutional by virtue of his own interpretation. "Aid" by a state agency to a religious enterprise is unconstitutional.

This earlier interpretation of Mr. Black was challenged in the brief of the lawyers for the Appellee in the Champaign case as merely *obiter dicta,* or incidental observations which have no binding force on subsequent decisions. Mr. Black, in his decision, rather sharply denied this contention, and maintained that his was the official constitutional doctrine: that no form of "aid" may be given, directly or indirectly, by a State or Federal agency to religion or religious education.

It is clear that this is a completely new constitutional doctrine, based uniquely on the personal opinions of the Justices themselves, and not on history or precedent. Moreover, it is clear that it is intended to be the precedent on which will be based the flood of new cases which will inevitably follow.

In his decision, Mr. Black repeated Thomas Jefferson's metaphor about the "wall" between church and state, but gratuitously reinforced it by stating that this wall should be kept "high and impregnable." In his concluding sentence, moreover, he inserted these ominous words:

"Here are not only the State's tax-supported public-school buildings used for the dissemination of religious doctrines. The State also affords sectarian groups an invaluable aid in that it helps to provide pupils for their classes through use of the State's compulsory public-school machinery. This is not separation of church and state."

What use will be made by the enemies of religion of this broad statement, in order to drive out of our public life all co-operation between our state and religion, it is impossible to predict.

What unelected public officials, but possessing great political strength, can effect on the course of American history, even though they are not endowed with legislative powers, is well illustrated in Justice Frankfurter's opinion, which ranks somewhat lower than the decision of the Court, though definitely higher than a mere concurring opinion.

Mr. Frankfurter begins by invoking, not the First Amendment, but "the constitutional principle of separation of church and state." He remarks that Illinois "authorized the commingling of religious with secular instruction in the public schools." And he adds: "The Constitution of the United States forbids this." Thereafter, however, after a mere routine reference to the First and Fourteenth Amendments, he speaks only of the "constitutional principle" of separation, though nowhere does he attempt to show where this is in the Constitution.

Mr. Frankfurter's opinion, however, will probably be known to history because of a new doctrine which he proposes for the construction of the Constitution, and which must be added to the several doctrines enumerated above.[1] It is, frankly, the doctrine of evolution. A "constitutional principle," like separation of church and state, is, according to him, "unfolded as appeal is made to the principle from case to case." Thus, he is completely able to evade the historical and constitutional argument, so painstakingly built up by the Appellee in the McCollum case. What was said there was

[1] See Chapter 5.

true in 1789, of course, and in 1845, but not, apparently, in 1948. Our *principles* seem to have evolved, and now mean something much different from what they once meant.

Mr. Frankfurter devotes seventeen pages to a long essay on the history of education in this country (with a side glance at anti-clerical France), and these pages are filled with learned footnotes, not quoting constitutional lore, as might be expected, but educational literature. His research in this field, however, is not, and could not be, a complete history of American educational theories, but only of that part of it which tends to confirm his own theory of what educational practice should be. It is on this partial survey that he confidently bases what he calls "the constitutional principle of separation" as it concerns the schools. As has been well said, "one finds in it the ideology and even the phraseology of a particular, partisan theory of law and philosophy of education, which now, it would seem, are to become doctrine in the United States by being written into our constitutional law." [2]

This amazing, one might almost say shattering, development may have incalculable consequences. Some of these are hinted at by Justice Jackson in

[2] John Courtney Murray, in NCWC News Service, March 15, 1948.

his concurring opinion. He criticizes severely the Court's sweeping directions to the Illinois Supreme Court in sustaining the plaintiff's complaint without discrimination. He says they are a "danger signal" which warns of the kind of local controversy the Court will be required to arbitrate. And he adds: "If we are to eliminate everything that is objectionable to these warring sects or inconsistent with any of their doctrines, we will leave public education in shreds." Later, he makes his position clearer: he holds that to do what the Court's decision, as he interprets it, would compel it to do, "is to allow zeal for our own ideas of what is good in public instruction to induce us to accept the role of a super-board of education for every school district in the nation." And he closes with a paragraph beginning with these devastating words: "It is idle to pretend that this task is one for which we can find in the Constitution one word to help us as judges to decide where the secular ends and the sectarian begins in education."

That would seem to dispose of Mr. Frankfurter's elaborate theory of education in the courts. Strangely, however, Mr. Jackson "joined" in the Frankfurter opinion, along with Justices Rutledge and Burton. More strangely still, perhaps, he "concurred" with the decision of the Court itself, yet in less than two pages he smashed the contention of the Court to bits. He is arguing that the Court had a doubtful jurisdiction in the Champaign case in the first place; and of course, a doubtful jurisdiction is no jurisdiction. His argument, briefly, is this: "A Federal Court may interfere with local school authorities only when they invade either a personal liberty or a property right protected by the Federal Constitution." He then proceeds to show that no personal liberty was involved in the case; neither was any measurable property right. His obvious conclusion is, therefore, that the Supreme Court had no right to take on this case for adjudication. An equally obvious conclusion, which, however, Mr. Jackson does not explicitly draw, would seem to be that the Champaign Plan was not against the Constitution.

Some light relief is afforded in the various opinions by the juggling which the Justices did with Thomas Jefferson's famous metaphor of "a wall of separation between church and state." Mr. Black had originally introduced this in the Everson case, and he relies heavily on it here. Mr. Frankfurter ends his opinion with these words: "If nowhere else, in the relation between church and state 'good fences make good neighbors.'" He does not say whether to have good neighbors there should be gates in those fences. Mr. Black, on the other hand, insists that the wall be kept "high and impregnable." Mr. Jackson predicts that, as a result of the many cases to come as a result of this decision, "we are likely to make the 'wall of separation between church and state' as winding as the famous serpentine wall designed by Mr. Jefferson for the university he founded." Whereupon, Justice Reed in his dissent drily remarks: "A rule of law should not be drawn from a figure of speech."

Justice Reed's dissent is remarkable in that he is the only one of the entire Court who took seriously the long historical and constitutional argument of the Appellees in the McCollum case, in which they showed, as has also been attempted in this book, the real legal meaning of the First Amendment. Mr. Black had dismissed that 168-page document with a few curt words in less than two lines, without further argument.

Mr. Reed assumes that those clauses of the First Amendment having to do with religion retain their historical meaning: there shall be no establishment by law; there shall be free exercise of religion. On this basis, he finds that the interpretation of the First Amendment in the decision and the two opinions is "erroneous." In fact, he confesses that "it is difficult to extract from the opinions any conclusion as to what it is in the Champaign Plan that is unconstitutional." It is not hard to see why he had this difficulty, since the opinions did not base their decision on the Constitution, but on a subjective norm called a "constitutional principle."

Mr. Reed then goes on to say that, "as no issue of prohibition upon the free exercise of religion is before us," the decision, to have any validity at all, must have been based on the no-establishment clause. He is unable to see how the Champaign Plan was an establishment of religion in the constitutional sense. In fact, while he allows that the concept has broadened with the years, this is the first time, he says, that the Court held "that recognition of the interest of our nation in religion, through the granting to qualified representatives of the principal faiths of opportunity to present religion as an optional, extracurricular subject during released school time in public-school buildings, was equivalent to an establishment of religion." Mr. Reed does not believe that it is equivalent.

Of Mr. Black's contention, first stated in a court by him in the Everson case, and cited by him here as a precedent, that the First Amendment forbids any "aid" to any or all religions—it all depends, says Mr. Reed, on what is meant by "aid," and on what is "aided." He agrees that the direct main-

173

tenance of church buildings and of worship in them is forbidden, but he excludes from the category of forbidden aid "those incidental advantages that religious bodies, with other groups similarly situated, obtain as a by-product of organized society" and he lists tax exemptions, free bus transportation, free textbooks, school lunches, and the like. Similarly, he cannot see that the various plans of co-operation between the public schools and religion are "aid" in the forbidden sense.

He adds a new item to the general picture: the compulsory chapel and prayers at West Point and Annapolis for Protestants, Jews, and Catholics, in chapels on the Academies' grounds, under the direction of chaplains. Are these now to be declared unconstitutional, along with the chaplains and prayers in Congress and the armed forces? There is certainly some "aid" to religion in these.

Mr. Reed says enough to make it clear that all such forms of indirect aid to religion, especially through the schools, cannot fairly be called an establishment of religion. This is the first time that a member of the Court has clarified the hitherto vague and all-inclusive concept of "aid to religion," and future court cases will undoubtedly profit by this in a more clear-cut definition.

Another original contribution made by Mr. Reed

has to do with the much-discussed position of Thomas Jefferson and James Madison with regard to our constitutional tradition. That position was the burden of Justice Rutledge's dissent in the Everson case, and much was made of it in the McCollum case. It will be remembered that the private ideas of the two great Virginians were made the basis of a new interpretation of the First Amendment itself, as forbidding all connection between tax-supported schools and religion.

Mr. Reed has now exhumed from the writings of Jefferson a most interesting, and it may be hoped a conclusive, instance. On October 7, 1822, Jefferson, as Rector of the University of Virginia, then as now a State-supported institution, made his annual report to the President and Directors of the Literary Fund, approved by the Board of Visitors, of which Madison was a member. In this report, Jefferson bewailed the fact that "the want of instruction in the various creeds of religious faith existing among our citizens presents . . . a chasm in a general institution of the useful sciences." Jefferson suggested an ingenious "remedy" for this chasm, and it was that the various sects be invited to establish their religious schools within the confines of the university, so that the undergraduates could also have the benefit of religious instruction and worship. Thus, said Jefferson, "the circle of the useful sciences embraced by this institution" would be completed, and the sacred right of freedom of religion would remain inviolate.[3] The suggestion was duly adopted by the university, and included in its statutes, to the effect that "the students of the university will be free and expected to attend religious worship at the establishment of their respective sects, in the morning, and in time to meet their school at the university at its stated hour."

Of this incident, Mr. Reed remarks: "Thus the 'wall of separation between church and state' that Mr. Jefferson built at the university which he founded did not exclude religious education from that school. The difference between the generality of his statements on the separation of church and state and the specificity of his conclusions on education are considerable." Mr. Reed clinches the argument, so far as Madison is concerned, by remarking: "Thus Mr. Madison's approval of Mr. Jefferson's report as Rector gives, in my opinion, a clearer indication of his views on the constitutionality of religious education in public schools than his general statements on a different subject."

Neither Jefferson nor Madison, after all, con-

[3] *The Writings of Thomas Jefferson* (Memorial Edition, 1904), Vol. 19, pp. 408, 409, 414-417, 449.

sidered that separation of church and state included separation of religion from education. Let us hope that we have heard the last of them as upholders of this latter kind of separation.

If we are to sum up this last chapter in the discussion, we are driven to the following conclusions:

(1) The present position of the Supreme Court is no longer based on the First and Fourteenth Amendments. In their place has been substituted a "constitutional principle" of separation of church and state, which it holds has evolved, and no doubt will evolve further, in the direction of complete secularism.

(2) This being so, the Court's method is no longer judicial, based on legal and constitutional provisions and decisions, but frankly legislative. It interprets church-state relations on what it considers to be wise and prudent, as legislators do, not on what is the law of the nation.

(3) Furthermore, it has injected itself into what are essentially local or regional arrangements, made by communities of citizens for the conducting of their schools. This is a much greater encroachment on local rights in favor of Federal centralism than has hitherto been made, and, if not checked, may have disastrous consequences.

(4) The no-establishment clause of the First

Amendment has now been extended to the States through the Fourteenth Amendment, though the Court gave no signs of having seriously considered the weighty legal arguments against that position adduced by the Appellee. Moreover, this clause is now given an almost indefinite possibility of extension.

(5) The freedom-of-religion clause also has been given a peculiar twist. Previous cases under this clause dealt with the rights of individuals and minorities as against the *state*. This case was different. It was a matter of one child and its parent as against all the other children in the community. It was decided in favor of the one child, but in this kind of case, what, it can be asked, becomes of the freedom of religion of all others? Before, it was always the power of the state that was restricted. Here, it is the freedom of other individual citizens that is denied. One can also legitimately wonder what becomes of the rights of taxpayers if they are forced to support a thoroughly secularized system to which in conscience they cannot adhere.

In conclusion, one can only say that, in view of its inherent contradictions, the McCollum case has not ended the controversy over separation of church and state. It is only beginning.

WITHDRAWN